I have known the founders of Our Sorrowful Mother's Ministry for many years and highly recommend their ministry. So many have been blessed over the years by this work, especially for the many souls in need of healing!
Fr. Vince Huber, FSSP

Our Sorrowful Mother's Ministry is a place for deeper prayer, healing, conversion and spiritual growth. The most frightful evil of our time is displacement of God and diminishment of prayer. Under the patronage of Our Lady of Sorrows, this ministry seeks to bring souls into an ever deeper union with the Most Holy Trinity and a more profound interior life. "The Kingdom of God is within you," says Our Blessed Lord.
Fr. Joseph Kuhlman

OSMM has helped others encounter the healing mercy of God for 25 years. We thank God for the desire for holiness and zeal for the Lord this ministry has instilled in its speakers, guests and retreatants. May He continue to bless OSMM and all associated with it. **Fr. Seth Brown**, *Chaplain of OSMM*

Debbie and Vanessa are amazing! When they said their fiat to follow God's call and founded Our Sorrowful Mother's Ministry, they opened the path to countless miracles of healing and reconciliation. They and their wonderful ministry are a true light in these dark times."
Msgr. Stuart Swetland, *President of Donnelly College, Kansas City, Kansas*

In the name of the Betania Spiritual Movement, I would like to congratulate you for these past 25 years of service to the

Lord and his Church. Your apostolate has benefited thousands of souls, providing a beautiful forum of healing, conversion, spiritual growth, catechetical formation and a deeper solidarity with the Catholic Church. Your work has taken a variety of forms reminiscent of the words of the great evangelist, St. Paul, who "was all things to all men." We give thanks to the Lord for this gift of your ministry that he has given to the People of God. May he strengthen, inspire, sustain, and provide for all of your needs so that your apostolate will thrive for years to come. May the Servant of God Maria Esperanza bless and protect you always.
Fr. Timothy E. Byerley*, Ph.D. Vice Postulator Beatification Cause of Maria Esperanza Medrano de Bianchini*

I have been hearing about the Our Sorrowful Mother's Ministry for a few years now from people in the Diocese of Rockford. People talk about their experiences and how they encountered the Lord's healing love through the events that they attended at their center in Vandalia, IL. When Bishop Paprocki opened the door for me to be able to practice my priestly ministry in the Diocese of Springfield, I paid a visit to Our Sorrowful Mother's Ministry Center and there, firsthand, I encountered what I have been hearing from people. It's a very special place. Their love for priests is extraordinary. Their hospitality is wonderful. It truly is a place of prayer and healing. Thank you for your generosity in sharing God's healing love. Thank you for letting us experience Our Sorrowful Mother's love and protection. Congratulations on your 25th Anniversary of service to God's people, to Holy Mother Church.
Fr. Erwin Caliente

"My soul magnifies the Lord, my spirit rejoices in God my Savior. For He had done great things in me and holy is His

name!" Fiat is the name of this book and fiat is the world that Vanessa and Debbie have spoken constantly, verbally and in their actions over these 25 years! I have heard it, seen it, witnessed it, in their joys, their laughter in their blood, sweat and tears. These two women have shown perseverance, courage, humility in that lived out word and we can see now more than ever that their works, words and love magnify our Lord. They have proven and Our Sorrowful Mother's ministry attests that they, like our Mother are the handmaids of the Lord! May the next 25 years see an explosion of joy, peace and fruitfulness!
Sr. Susan Pieper

The graces that Our Lord has given through Our Lady these last 25 years are innumerable! As a Vandalia native, and the first priest ordained for our diocese from Mother of Dolors, it has been so beautiful to see the fruit borne in so many souls through OSMM and our parish. Under the guidance of long-time pastor Fr. Steve Sotiroff, all our foundations were built on solid rock: Eucharistic Adoration, frequent confession, recognizing how great a need we all have for the Lord's healing mercy, and unwavering zeal for handing on the Truth. In today's spiritual battle, I cannot urge the faithful enough to seek refuge and peace with Our Lady at OSMM!
Fr. Zach Edgar *Native son & Chapluin of the Illinois Veterans Home at Quincy*

In the Gospel of John we are told that the wind blows where it will. This wind, the Spirit, is alive and well in the small town of Vandalia, Illinois. For the last 25 years, Our Sorrowful Mother's Ministry has been a sanctuary and refuge against the false gods of this world. Here at OSMM the Spirit of love and truth, of peace and promise, and of healing and reconciliation have found a home. Here at OSMM the Spirit of the Lord has been set free "to bring glad tidings to the poor...to proclaim liberty to captives and recovery of sight to the blind, to let the oppressed go free." Here at OSMM faith has been reignited, hope has been restored, and love has been realized.

To Debbie and Vanessa and the entire OSMM community, thank you for your "Yes" to the promptings of the Spirit. Despite the tremendous sacrifice and suffering along the way, or maybe because of it, this ministry has been a source of tremendous grace and mercy for so many. May God continue to pour out His blessings and save souls through Our Sorrowful Mother's Ministry for another 25 years!
John LaBriola, *Author and Catholic Speaker*

Fiat

By Debbie Pryor and Vanessa Keck

Our Sorrowful Mother's Ministry,
Vandalia, IL

Copyright 2022
Debbie Pryor and Vanessa Keck
ISBN: 9798849476377

Scripture texts in this work are taken from the *New American Bible, revised edition* © 2010, 1991, 1986, 1970 Confraternity of Christian Doctrine, Washington, D.C. and are used by permission of the copyright owner. All Rights Reserved. No part of the New American Bible may be reproduced in any form without
permission in writing from the copyright owner.

*Dedicated to Fr. Peter Mary Rookey, OSM, and all the priests
who have shared their priestly ministry at OSMM*

This story took a very long time to tell, and Ann sat with us and wrote down all of our memories and miracles and assembled it all into a cohesive story.
Ann is the key to this written labor of love.

Introduction

Our Sorrowful Mother's Ministry is situated in the town of Vandalia within Fayette County, Illinois. Many people like to refer to this as the middle of nowhere or flyover territory. Vandalia is a small town of approximately 7000 people, including the local prison population. Fayette County is less than 3% Catholic so it is surprising that a Catholic ministry would even exist here. You can find Vandalia about 60 miles due east of St. Louis along Interstate 70. The proximity of the interstate highway at least makes it accessible for traveling, albeit long distances from any large city.

As has commonly proven to be the case when God wants to send a message, He does so through the least likely of sources. Consider how apparitions have occurred over the centuries with the little girl Bernadette at Lourdes, the poor peasant Juan Diego of Guadalupe or the young children who were the shepherds of Fatima. We are like the little children who saw the apparitions of Our Lady. We see, feel, know and experience her every day.

By God's initiation, we were chosen. We are not

qualified or worthy of any of it. This commitment is a gift from God that we embrace. Our work is all for the Glory of God. We have maintained the great "Fiat" when we didn't even know what saying "yes" meant. In Fatima, Our Lady asked the seers, *"Will you offer yourselves to God and bear all the sufferings He sends you?"* They said yes with no understanding of the sacrifices they would make. We do not claim that our sacrifices match theirs, but sacrifice is tantamount to the virtue of love. To love is to will the good of another, to love our neighbor as ourselves. We are all challenged to put aside our needs and wants and submit to the will of God. We have been asked over and over again for our "yes." It will be our reply to each call that God makes of us. We are led to not think about ourselves too much but to keep our hearts alert to the Voice of God. To do God's work, we have to respond to these calls with a firm yes. We are not called to just be comfortable where we are but to press forward into the unknown and untried. Our motto is *Ad Serviam*, I will serve.

Despite the odds, a small ministry in the middle of nowhere has been able to survive and thrive for 25 years bringing world-renowned priests and speakers to teach, preach and evangelize. God used two women who were re-awakening in their faith and exploded it into a ministry that brings hundreds of people every year and has changed the lives of countless souls.

As a drop of a pebble in the water spreads out in a circular form and increases in size, the people who have come here have traveled home throughout the United States and literally throughout the world and taken the message of God with them.

Only in the next life will we know how actions taken or omitted or words spoken or unspoken changed others' lives forever.

This is the story of Our Sorrowful Mother's Ministry and the founders: Debbie Pryor and Vanessa Keck who allowed Our Lord and Our Lady to lead them on an incredible journey.

Chapter 1

Our Stories

Debbie's Journey

In the mid-90s, I had suffered through some life-altering personal losses. Trying to find out the answers to difficult questions, I started to look back at the faith of my childhood. I began to speak to a friend named Cheryl, and we met regularly, discussing the losses, pain and circumstances I now found myself in. We would meet at her house and talk for hours.

I was working for my dad as the service manager of his car dealership and knew Vanessa as a customer. At times, when Vanessa came in seeking service work, she noticed I was sad or upset. We would talk briefly, and I began to share and confide in her.

Vanessa was also acquainted with my friend, Cheryl, who was slowly drawing me closer to the faith. Vanessa's and Cheryl's children were friends, and they had shared activities together, taking the kids to different outings. She was also having a re-awakening of her faith.

Cheryl encouraged the friendship between Vanessa and myself. At the same time, I knew in my heart that I was to be friends with Vanessa. I started to call her and invite her to local religious events. We would go together as mutual acquaintances, but I felt in my heart that we would be on a journey together that exceeded mere friendship. I am forever grateful to Cheryl for listening to the promptings of the Holy Spirit that led her to encourage the friendship between Vanessa and myself.

Eventually, in 1996, Vanessa and I traveled out of town to attend a Marian conference. The trip inspired us to start the wheels in motion to have a conference here in our town to bring the faith to our friends and fellow parishioners. Living in a predominantly Protestant area made attending Catholic events to grow in the faith difficult. Our initial goal was to share the fire that was growing in us for the Catholic faith with our parish.

I see Vanessa as the inner soul of the ministry in every way. We have completely different personalities but find a way to work together as a team. Vanessa manages the finances and is the detail person who arranges air travel for speakers, list of retreatants, does all of our shipping and generally everything to keep the lights on. She is the "strong, silent giant" behind the scenes keeping it all together. She is a true, loyal friend who would do anything for me without considering the cost for herself.

Vanessa's Journey
The story of the birth of OSMM was not like being knocked down by a bolt of lightning as St. Paul experienced, but in a way, it really was like that. Debbie and I became friends around 1995 through a mutual friend and began attending religious events and conferences together. This all sounds pretty simplistic, but if you knew me back in 1995, I was a tough nut to crack. I was very quiet, reserved and when people hugged me, it was similar to grabbing hold of a board, a very hard board. I was not very approachable. If you know Debbie, she was going to have none of that, and for her, hugging is the name of the game, BIG hugging.

She was known far and wide for her hugs, but I did not care to be a recipient. Unbeknownst to me, God was telling her that we must be friends, and she was bound and determined to make that happen. I, on the other hand, was very perplexed as to why she kept calling me and asking me to go here and there. That was not at all how I operated, but I went along with it anyway, albeit kicking and screaming.

The background story here is important as this was most definitely a friendship ordained by God. Left to our own devices, we probably would not have become close friends. We are as opposite as we can be in just about all ways except in the ways of God. We were and are always striving for holiness and truth, no matter how distant that may be.

In 1996, as we continued along our spiritual journey, one of our road trips was to a Marian conference. We were at the point where we needed spiritual nourishment, and so we went there to obtain it. Much to our disappointment, we left there still starving. On the ride home, as we were talking, which we did a lot, and expressing our letdown, Debbie said, "Let's do our own conference, and we will do it right." I was stunned and excited at the same time. My first words were, "in Vandalia?" Remember, the entire county is less than three percent Catholic. Against all odds we forged ahead with Debbie leading the charge and my head still spinning.
There were no plans to begin a ministry and make

this our life's work. We felt inspired to do something to spread the faith and little did we know where that would take us.

OSMM absolutely could not operate without the expertise of Debbie Pryor. God certainly knew what He was doing; imagine that? Debbie is the engine that drives it and she is unafraid to step out and do the things that others would not. She spends months and hours on end researching, calling and scheduling the outstanding speakers that have been our hallmark since the very beginning. You will not find a better roster of speakers, even in the largest venues. The cream of the crop has been here, and many, on more than one occasion.

If someone tells her, you will never be able to get them, she basically says, "watch me." She cowers under nothing but forges full steam ahead. One reason we have not been able to have some priests and presenters here is because their stipend is too prohibitive, not because she was unable to book them. She has literally chased priests at other conferences and events we've gone to, to speak to them about coming here.

She does many other things in addition to scheduling speakers, like being the shoulder to cry on for hundreds of people and offering consolation and direction. The stool sitting next to her chair at the Sanctuary is famous. Many line up to speak with her or get one of her Mama Bear hugs.

Debbie was told long ago by several priests that she has the gift of healing. She always saw that as placing her hands (and they are hot ones!) on people for their intention but she did not feel called to do that. What she eventually learned was that her healing gift is her hugs, her warmth & her generosity for people. God had a very special purpose in this life for Debbie and she fulfills it in abundance.

Chapter 2

God Prepares Us for Our Mission

Fr. Peter Mary Rookey, OSM

About this time, a set of circumstances occurred that would set God's plan in motion. The secretary from our parish, Mother of Dolors, called Debbie and asked her if she knew anything about a priest named Fr. Rookey. She had received a call from someone asking about him and did not know how to respond. Neither Debbie nor Vanessa had ever heard of Fr. Rookey, but providentially the very next day, Debbie received a flyer in the mail promoting Fr. Rookey's healing Masses in the St. Louis parishes of St. Norbert and Mary, Queen of the Universe. Debbie immediately called Vanessa, and off they went to the healing Masses.

We went to our first Mass with Fr. Rookey and were hooked. We continued to attend these Masses one weekend each month when Fr. Rookey came to St Louis for First Saturday weekends.
The monthly routine was that Fr. Rookey would celebrate a healing Hass on the morning of First

Saturday at the Basilica of Our Lady of Sorrows in Chicago which was served by his order, the Servants of Mary. He would fly to St. Louis and celebrate Mass at St. Norbert in North County on Saturday night. On Sunday morning, he visited the sick in homes, hospitals, nursing homes and wherever he was requested. In the afternoon, he celebrated Mass at Mary, Queen of the Universe in South County. These healing services had a profound effect on everyone who attended. We witnessed a truly holy priest praying the Mass and then praying over each person who was there. It didn't matter how long it took or what was asked of him; Fr. Rookey took the time to accommodate all requests for prayer. Many times, people would "rest in the spirit" and receive the emotional, spiritual or physical healing they were seeking. In his great humility, Fr. Rookey never accepted any credit or gratitude for the blessings people received. He always, without fail, gave all the glory to God. "I do nothing," he would say, "God heals," with his arms raised to heaven.

Within a few months, we were asked by his St. Louis coordinator to take over for her when Fr. Rookey was in St. Louis. This came as quite the surprise as we lived over an hour away, and it involved late hours and then returning the next morning until late afternoon one weekend every month. It was especially odd because there were many faithful followers of Fr. Rookey, who attended these Masses religiously, lived in St Louis, and would have jumped at this chance. But, Geneva, the coordinator, said she knew it was supposed to be us, and so we readily accepted.

On each First Saturday weekend, after taking appointments for visits to the sick for Fr. Rookey, we began by arriving early to set up tables with all of Fr. Rookey's wares for sale: books, holy oil, recordings and rosaries. (We would meet him at St. Norbert's) Packing everything up before Mass began, then followed by the Mass and healing service. We waited for Fr Rookey to finish speaking with the many people surrounding him. Any time someone handed Fr. Rookey a gift, he would thank them and just as quickly hand it off to someone else who might want it. He never kept anything given to him. People always wanted to whisk him away to see this one or that one, so Debbie acted as his bouncer and had to step in to protect him as his answer to everyone about everything was "yes." Debbie's answer to those people was "no." Father would have been up all night with no rest if the crowds had had their way. This was all happening very late into the evening, but it did not matter to them. Geneva had told us that above all, we must protect Fr. Rookey, as everyone wanted a piece of him, and if you allow it, there will be nothing left. After that, we would drive Father to Seven Holy Founders in South St. Louis, where he would spend the night in the rectory.

Driving the 60-plus miles, we would arrive home at about one a.m. On Sunday morning, we would get up, go back to Seven Holy Founders, where we had left just a few short hours before, and have coffee and talk. Fr. Rookey never tired or appeared fatigued. He often fasted for much of the day, commonly only eating one meal.

From there, we escorted Father to the many appointments he had at peoples' homes and hospitals to pray over them and bless them. There were visits to make until it was time to head for Mary, Queen of the Universe, in South County, for the Servite Rosary and another healing Mass. Again, tables were set up to provide his CDs and other goods to sell.

At the end of day, we would take him back to the

airport to fly back to Chicago until next month. Over all the years we knew Fr. Rookey, he would always thank us and send us home with his blessing. He would "tuck us in" by saying goodbye and, while closing the car door, tell us, "you girls go straight home now." He would wave with a two-finger peace sign until we were out of sight.

To some, accompanying Fr. Rookey month after month would appear to be a burden, but to us, it was a great privilege to assist such a holy and humble priest. We centered our lives on serving his ministry and learning from him as a mentor. Our journey with him was guided by the Holy Spirit, and the desire to serve with him was compelling. Anything we had to do with our families or personal lives took a back seat to "Fr. Rookey" weekends. God cleared the path for us to learn and grow in our faith through the witness of this humble priest. It was a sacred and treasured time for both of us. Our families supported and encouraged us. We are grateful for this grace.

For Fr. Rookey, everything was rooted in humility and obedience, giving God all the glory for whatever miracles happened. He was truly Jesus, "another Christ" to everyone, no matter the faith or circumstances. Interestingly enough, the 'Fr. Rookey weekends' ended about the time we were expanding the retreats we were hosting. One endeavor ended to allow the beginning of the next step of our journey.

Many people inquire as to what miracles we have seen working with Fr. Rookey. We believe the first miracle was that we were called to that position in the first place. Then we tell the people that the Masses and rosaries we participated in and the sheer time we were able to spend with him were a second miracle.

Of course, they are referring to things like healing the lame and giving sight to the blind. The healing miracles with Fr. Rookey usually happened after the fact. We would hear of all kinds of healing: physical, spiritual and emotional. Often, people would see the face of Jesus in the Holy Eucharist, or there would be a strong aroma of roses in the air during the healing services. We were privileged to accompany Father as his assistants for six years.

On May 19, 2007, we held an anniversary event for Fr. Rookey. He was able to travel from Chicago to Vandalia in honor of his 66th anniversary of ordination. Over 100 people were in attendance. Father offered Mass and led the Servite Rosary in Mary's Chapel at the House of Bethany.

That same year, Fr. Rookey told us, "the Finger of God is on this ministry." A few months later, Sr. Susan used those same words, though we had not shared that with her. It was confirmed two more times by other people who said the same thing.

In 2010, we wanted to honor Fr. Rookey by inviting him to go on a pilgrimage to the Holy Land. At 93 years old, it was to be his last trip there. We secured a sponsor for the trip and hired Chuck Neff and Salt River Production Group to record the trip. Father led us and a group of about 40 people throughout the Holy Land, and everywhere we went, people knew him. From ordinary people to many Franciscans, people stopped to talk and visit with him. One of the truly holy moments was when Fr. Rookey led us in prayer as we walked the Via Dolorosa at daybreak. It was truly a blessing. Another incident was at the Milk Grotto. When our group arrived, it was closed for the noon hour. As we turned to leave, a Franciscan priest came out, recognized Fr. Rookey and promptly let us in for a tour. It was amazing how many people just wanted to talk to him and would do anything to help him.

Catholic singer Annie Karto accompanied us on this trip, and one of the most beautiful scenes was Annie singing "Pilgrimage of Love" to Fr. Rookey on the shores of the Lake of Galilee. Father was visibly moved and completely humbled by the love outpoured on him during this trip.

As Fr. Rookey grew older and became more frail, he no longer came to St. Louis for Masses, but he still continued his phone ministry in Chicago. We would regularly refer friends to Father, and he would call and pray with them. We stayed in contact with Father by phone and would go to see him regularly in Chicago to care for him, listen to his stories and keep him company. When he was not able to continue his public ministry, he longed for human contact, and we would visit him to spend time talking and supporting him. He was our friend and mentor, and we would never abandon him.

The last earthly blessings given to Fr. Rookey was when he died on September 10, 2014, on the feast day of St. Nicholas of Tolentino, Patron of Holy Souls, with his funeral mass being held on September 15,

2014, the Feast of Our Lady of Sorrows to whom he had dedicated his priesthood.

While we were at his funeral, the Prior of his order told us to go to Father's room and take whatever we wanted. There was not much left by this time, as thankfully, Fr. Rookey had already given us most of his personal items from his ministry.

We sat right in the first row and watched the many mourners come up and bewail the fact he was gone. We were sad that he was no longer with us but so happy for Father that he was right where he wanted to be. We would tell Father often while he was alive that when he got to heaven, we would be holding on to his coat tails, and he should throw down a rope for us to climb.

It was a beautiful funeral held at the Basilica of Our Lady of Sorrows in Chicago, which Father loved and cherished.

Fr. Tom McCarthy
Another chapter at the beginning of our journey involved meeting Fr. Tom McCarthy, a Viatorian priest who experienced a Eucharistic miracle while celebrating mass in a chapel with Audrey Santo in

Worcester, MA. This was in 1997, long before she became well known and the crowds descended on their house. After that, you could no longer go near Little Audrey or even be in the room but could only look through a glass partition. Fr. McCarthy invited us to go to that chapel and visit with Audrey, a little girl who was left incapacitated by a near-drowning accident. We visited the chapel with him, met Audrey and her mother. We sat with Audrey, touching her hand and asking for her intercession for our intentions. Audrey's condition left her unable to speak and with little voluntary movement, but her mind was active and aware. We were the only ones present, and when Fr. Tom approached the bed, she responded to him. She was very drawn to and aware of priests. Many sacred images were within the chapel and Audrey's room, and they all had a little plastic cup under them to catch the oil exuding from the images.

We developed a friendship with Fr. McCarthy and often visited him in the Chicago area. Father eventually became ill with cancer, and we would visit him in a home for priests in Arlington Heights. Father was very proud of his Irish heritage and had a small mechanical leprechaun that played music.

Before we would visit, he would wind up the leprechaun and place it in the hall outside his room so it would greet us as we arrived. He would play his fiddle for us while we visited. He was a kind and gentle priest. As he declined, he asked us to take care of all the items he had associated with Audrey Santo after he passed. Interestingly, Fr. Rookey asked us to do the same with many of his personal items at the same time. Currently, we have a small room in our Sanctuary dedicated to Fr. Rookey, which contains many of his personal artifacts from his ministry. We have a cabinet dedicated to Fr. Tom McCarthy with displays of his personal items, including the violin he loved to play whenever he had an opportunity, including playing it at the nursing home for other residents.

In particular, Fr. McCarthy wanted us to safeguard a ring he had received when he was ordained a priest of the Viatorian order. The ring was too big for him to wear as he had lost so much weight, and it would no longer stay on his finger. Shortly before his death, he told us he wanted to be buried with the ring and asked us to help him. Of course, we agreed and asked Father to remember us with prayers when he was in heaven. After Fr. McCarthy's death, a Prior from his order called us and asked for the ring. We refused to give it to him, citing our promise to Fr. Tom. We conferred with a priest we knew, and he advised us to keep our promise and not return the ring to the order. At the wake for Fr. Tom, the Prior again asked us for the ring. We refused as we were determined to keep our promise. As the funeral directors prepared to close the casket for the final time, we approached and knelt down on the kneeler. Whenever anyone did something for Fr. Tom, he would respond, "Thank you, thank you very much." As we spoke our final prayers, we told Fr. Tom, "Thank you, thank you very much," and we placed the ring on his finger, and the promise was kept. Fr. Tom was a good and holy priest who had a profound influence on us. God was with us again on every step of our journey.

During these early years, we met Judy Brown, who was working at Holy Angels Church in Kinloch, Missouri. She and Fr. Ed Schramm worked with the poor parishioners in the area. Judy has many gifts, especially charismatic gifts of praying with others. She prayed with us and told us we were going to do 'something great for God.' Naturally, we had no idea what that meant. Judy spoke the first words to us about what God's plans were for our future. When Holy Angels closed, we received three large statues of the Archangels and a large statue of the Scourged Christ. They are among the many statues and church furnishings we have preserved from being lost. Judy has lived a life of the beatitudes, always serving others and has come to OSMM several times over the last 25 years when she has felt God calling her to do so. As we look back, we can see how God provides the people we need at the perfect time.

Chapter 3

The Journey of Our Sorrowful Mother's Ministry Begins

Our first event in 1997 was hosting Fr. Rookey at our own parish. Our only purpose was to share the great gift of Fr. Rookey and his healing ministry with our friends and fellow parishioners. Lots of people attended, both Catholic and non-Catholics.

Not having an official name yet, we were called "The Spiritual Life" by our pastor, Fr. Stephen Sotiroff. We held several small events in the next year. In 1998, we held our first Marian Conference asking for help from the people who had held the Marian Conference we had attended earlier. They assisted us by giving advice and choosing the speakers and topics for the conference. It was held at our local high school, and by all appearances, it went well. But somehow, it didn't feel right. We did not feel it was "us" or what we were trying to convey. We began to notice that other conferences seemed to have too much emphasis on money or secular concerns. We decided to go out on our own, following however God led us. We looked to Fr. Rookey as our spiritual father guiding us along the way.

The pastor of our local parish, Fr. Stephen Sotiroff, was instrumental in the beginning years of the ministry. We are very grateful for his invaluable support and advice in our early years, as we would not have been successful without his teaching and leading us. Fr. Steve arrived at the parish about the same time that we were both having a reversion to the faith. He was working hard as the pastor of our church to evangelize and catechize the local people. He was also involved with Marriage Encounter at the same time and had written some articles on marriage and family life for Marriage Encounter magazine. He was open to the ministry even though he had no idea how successful it would be. He felt it was what the church in general needed at that time as he desired to form people spiritually. While we were trying to evangelize, we were also being evangelized ourselves. Most of what we learned at the time was through Fr. Steve teaching us the basics of the faith, forming us in the faith, and giving us the firm foundation we needed to go forward.

Within the parish, Fr. Steve saw the exodus of our youth to other denominations because they were offering youth programs based on fun and friendship. While those are not evil in their own right, they were drawing our kids away from the true faith. He wanted to develop a program of catechesis for the adult members of the parish and for the youth. It consisted of catechetical formation and catechetical experiences. He was open to whatever would accomplish this for the good of the parish. This coincided with what we were trying to do with the ministry. The youth of our parish became involved, attending the retreats, helping out with providing daycare, serving Mass and other duties. With many people attending our events, including diocesan personnel and seminarians, it soon became part of their formation. He taught us to base all decisions on faith first. Everything else comes second.

Fr. Steve helped us by hosting priests who were speakers at the rectory. He drove them to and from the high school when they were speaking. He spoke at our events and advised us in all ways. We met with him regularly to discuss all types of problems. All of this extra work was in addition to all he had to do as our pastor. Fr. Steve ensured that our finances were kept separate from the parish. The accounting firm that was responsible for our church's finances maintained the records and publicly made the parishioners aware that OSMM was not being financed by the parish.

We have never received any funds from our parish, the diocese or any formal organization of the Catholic Church. We function solely on private donations. No one in OSMM receives a salary. Everyone is a volunteer, and many of them donate generously and regularly to the ministry. In addition, a number of people have received blessings and healings when they were at OSMM, and many have wanted to "pay back" by giving us donations for different items like statues and artwork.

During this time, we were privileged to have Archbishop Joseph Naumann speak at our conference, and then the next year, hosted by then-bishop of the Diocese of Springfield, George Lucas. Fr. Thomas Dubay came two years in a row. The Fathers of Mercy led many of our retreats and have become a mainstay in our ministry. In addition, our current bishop since 2010, Bishop Thomas John Paprocki , has spoken at our conference a number of times.

Fr Steve described OSMM as a grassroots movement laying the foundation as a legitimate healing ministry. It is a place where people who simply need prayer to correct the evil that has been done to them can receive it.

In 2005, Fr. Steve was reassigned, and we had lost our day-to-day support for the ministry.

He had given us the encouragement we needed to continue. He has a deep and reflective personality that sees beyond the immediate and looks to our ultimate goal; to become holy and reach heaven taking as many people with us as we can. Although he is no longer involved in our day-to-day endeavors, we can still go to him at any time, and he understands our struggles and always has solid advice for us.

As we were just beginning, we were advised by people in other ministries to have a steering committee and hold regular meetings, but that was not the way it would be. It has never been that way. We forged ahead, trusting God would provide the funds and people we needed to move forward. The Annual Conference grew, and the 'best of the best' speakers have been here as presenters. From the beginning, Debbie has been the person to procure every priest and every lay speaker. It is a time-intensive task that requires much research, many phone calls and hounding. If anyone knows how to hound, it is Debbie. Relentless is her middle name.

We decided to change our name to Our Sorrowful Mother's Ministry – or rather, it chose us. It was a natural choice since our home parish in Vandalia is called Mother of Dolors; *dolors* meaning sorrows in Latin. Fr. Rookey was a priest of the Servants of Mary who have the Sorrowful Mother as the principal devotion of their order. We wanted to honor Fr. Rookey since he was so important in our formation, and with his encouragement and blessing, we moved ahead with this endeavor for God. Interestingly enough, we felt drawn to Our Lady by her title of Mother of Sorrows as we saw such heartache in the world and knew Our Lady is our Refuge in Sorrow.

Five retreat weekends were held in 1998 in addition to the Annual Conference. It was the first of the Annual Conferences that continue until today. The ministry continued to grow rapidly. The following year, five more retreat weekends were held, with over 1500 people attending the Annual Conference. Our mission from the very beginning, aside from wanting our parish to know the truth of the Faith, was to minister to priests and offer consolation and protection when they needed it. Our earliest retreats and conferences centered on apologetics but has always included healing services.

The healing services were the reason many people came. They wanted to hear the talks but being prayed over by the priest was what they were seeking. Many Catholics are not aware of the charismatic gifts that are very present in the Catholic Church. People tend to think this is only something for Protestant groups like Pentecostals, Evangelicals or non-denominational groups. If they are familiar with them, they believe it is solely from the Charismatic Renewal that began at Duquesne University in 1967. That event may have brought a new awareness of the charisms, but Fr. Rookey and other priests had long been celebrating healing Masses.

During the healing service, the priest would pray over each person individually. They may anoint them with holy oil, place their hand on the head of the person and say a few words of prayer. Each person experienced whatever they were open to and what God intended for them. Some felt a wave of peace come over them, smelled the sweet aroma of roses or some other phenomena. Many people would "rest in the spirit." They would gently fall backward with "catchers" gently guiding them. It was an amazing occurrence that each person who was "slain in the spirit" could be guided downward most of the time with little effort. We had community members who would stand behind each person and be ready to catch them if necessary. People would literally lie on the floor for anywhere from a few minutes to several minutes while the spirit overtook them. Most people described it as a peaceful consolation from God.

The evenings concluded with people witnessing what they had experienced, often mentioning spiritual or emotional healing. People reported simple consolations or feelings of euphoria or, at times, deep childhood wounds that were healed.

Some of our benefactors have been people who had such a profound experience at our retreats that they wanted to show their gratitude by anonymously donating to our buildings or other projects. Because of the private nature of their woundedness, they often do not want any mention of their names. They had encountered God in an intimate personal way, and they felt safe and loved.

Prayer teams became a big part of the ministry experience. Time was set aside for people to meet with prayer teams and ask for prayer for themselves or others. Several teams of two or three community members would pray together with people. Sometimes people came with a specific intention for prayer, and other times they just came and asked for whatever the Holy Spirit had for them. For a while, we had a prayer team in the living room of Bethany House and one team in the chapel below. The lines to meet with prayer teams were long, but people waited up to a couple of hours at times to meet with the prayer teams because they wanted to receive the words that the Holy Spirit would speak through those who had prayed with them. It became a powerful part of the ministry. Once, Sue Young remarked about the prayer teams, "It is a Mount Zion experience–where man meets God." It is uncanny how God can use an empty vessel to fill the hearts of another. It was all God working through the ministry for those who were seeking Him. Many people have served as prayer team leaders through the years, and God has been the One who provided the right people at the right time.

God's Providence was at work once again when we contacted Dr. Kenneth Howell, who was a professor at the University of Illinois, to ask about spiritual direction. He connected us to Sr. Susan, who was a founding member of the Apostles of the Interior Life, and we began our lifetime friendship with her. Sr. Susan is originally from California but had studied in Rome and had recently arrived from Italy to begin work in an apostolate that teaches, encourages and provides growth in the interior life, primarily aimed at college-age students. She led us to Msgr. Stuart Swetland, who was the chaplain of the Newman Center at the University of Illinois. Msgr. Swetland presented a talk at our Annual Conference in 2001, and Sr. Susan accompanied him. We have counted on Msgr. Swetland from that day forward. He wears many hats in our lives; mentor, priest and beloved friend. He is always there, no matter what the issue is; to counsel and encourage us to take the next step. We know he has our back and is there to push us to succeed and not be discouraged. We love and respect him and are honored to have him as our friend.

Sr. Susan has been our spiritual director and our confidante for over 20 years. Since 2002, she has presented at every Annual Conference leading meditations that build the interior life. Even in 2020, when she was caring for her elderly parents in California, she spoke to the attendees via a live stream connection. Sr. Susan has stayed the course, opened the gates of our minds and souls with the love of our faith and our God. She has taken us deeper in the understanding of countless things as we walk this call to ministry, one step at a time. She has taught us that, with perseverance, we will gain our lives. But perseverance is tempered by discipline and order to have a balanced life. Susan is one of the people we call when the world is collapsing around us. We love and honor her. Our friendship goes beyond the worldly as we are kindred souls.

At first, OSMM events were held in various places, from our local church to the local high school and junior high school to Mother of Dolors Parish Center. As the ministry grew, so did the number of items needed to hold the retreats. In the first few years, through the support of our pastor, Fr. Stephen Sotiroff, we were able to use the church's liturgical items for Holy Mass, including vestments, the chalice and ciborium, altar cloths and other needed items.

We would have adoration all day during the conferences, and it was held in various places, including classrooms and even the school locker room. But before someone objects, you have to realize that we hold the Blessed Sacrament in the highest esteem. The room would be furnished and converted to prepare a place of great honor. Our pastor would bring the Blessed Sacrament and monstrance, and it was treated with the utmost reverence the entire time. The adoration time was always covered with our Lord being honored every moment of the conference and then returned by our pastor to our parish.

God was truly present during this time as we would reserve the local high school for our Annual Conference and for several days ahead of time to set up. This involved the students staying off the floor for P.E. classes while hundreds of chairs were set up. The custodians of the school would set up the stage used for graduation on one end of the gym, and above it hang huge banners from the girders of the gym ceiling. We had banners of the apparition at Fatima, the Blessed Sacrament and other religious symbols. All around the perimeter were crucifixes, statues and other items. The amazing thing to remember is this is a public high school in a predominantly Protestant town. We can only imagine what the students thought as they watched all the preparations take place. Besides the high school, we used the local junior high and even our own church's parish center for our events for nearly 15 years!

Over the next few years, we had to purchase all the liturgical items needed for Mass in addition to vestments, altar server robes, a monstrance, candles stands, liturgical books and pretty much all the items a church would have. We wanted to make the gymnasiums look more like a sacred space, so we purchased banners, backdrops, statues, crucifixes and prints to adorn the space. We started to offer books and sacramentals as a way to provide for the spiritual needs of our retreatants and to provide some income to support the ministry. We offered rosaries, statues, scapulars and many, many books. All of these items had to be stored between events. We used the garage at Bethany and rented a storage unit. This meant before each event, all of these items had to be transported to the event, set up and then re-packed and returned after the retreat was over. It was time-consuming and quite a physical ordeal as the books, statues and other items were bulky and heavy.

Our retreats and conferences continued for the next few years, when in 2005, Fr. Chris Crotty, who had presented several retreats and healing services for

OSMM advised us that we needed to have smaller, more intimate monthly retreats because people were yearning for a personal encounter. We have always followed the discernment of trusted priests, so our emphasis began to shift from apologetics to healing and reconciliation. We want to provide a venue where people can have a personal encounter with Our Lord and the Blessed Mother.

When we received this discernment from a trusted priest, we immediately followed it. It is why we relate to the word, "Fiat." We give our "yes" to however the Holy Spirit leads us.

We have continued with this format until the present. It has taken on some different nuances, but the basic goal is always healing and reconciliation. We aim to lead people into a personal encounter with God the Father, through Jesus, His Son and with the guidance of the Holy Spirit. In all of this, we rely on our Blessed Mother, especially in her Sorrows, to draw closer to Jesus. She is the most powerful intercessor as she brings all our prayers to perfection when she presents them to her Son.

Literally, hundreds of people have presented at our

events. The list is mind-boggling when you look through the names and realize how many bishops, priests and lay speakers have been here. It rivals any Catholic television/radio station, including EWTN. It has all been our privilege to meet and speak to these people. We sometimes wonder how different our lives would have been if we did not have the opportunity to listen, learn and share our faith with so many holy people. OSMM has been our lives' work. It consumes us on a daily level, but we would not have wished for any other life. It's been a blessing beyond anything we could have ever imagined for ourselves. Astonishingly enough, we have had people from all 50 states and from Canada attend our retreats. It is not unusual to have people from 10-15 different states for a single event. The cross-section of people from all walks of life who we have met has been a blessing. We get to learn about their lives as they share their stories with us.

A major change to OSMM occurred in 2011. As we continued to look for new speakers and topics, Debbie kept reading about the apparitions that had occurred in *Betania*, Venezuela since the 1980s. The main seer and mystic, Maria Esperanza, had passed away in 2004, but her husband, Geo Bianchini, and her family were actively promoting the message of Our Lady as she appeared in *Betania*. We were referred to Fr. Tim Byerley, who is the vice-postulator for the cause for Beatification of Maria Esperanza. Debbie contacted him, who in turn contacted the family. It was set up that Fr. Byerley and the family of Maria Esperanza would come in November 2011 to present a retreat on Maria Esperanza and the message of Our Lady, who came under the title of Reconciler of All Peoples and Nations. *Señor* Geo, the husband of Maria Esperanza, came with about six other family members and two members of the *Betania* foundation. All of these people had witnessed Our Lady in 1984, and the effect on them was transparent. They carried the love of Christ and Our Lady with them. They had many of the same mystical gifts as their mother. Maria Esperanza had the dream of *Betania* communities being set up throughout the world, praying for peace and reconciliation. Before the weekend was over, *Señor* Geo had conferred with his family, and they invited us to become the sixteenth *Betania* Community. One of the most remarkable events in Maria Esperanza's life was an incident where 16 roses emerged from her chest one at a time, so the number had a special significance. We were honored to accept their invitation to become *Betania* 16 and carry on the message of Our Lady. Señor Geo told us we were to be the "Beacon of Light" in the middle of the United States for all the faithful. We aim to be a Beacon of Light and give hope to people's hearts who are moved to come here to be renewed and refreshed, strengthened to go on among the Church Militant fighting for salvation.

They were able to return in 2013, 2015 and 2016 to give their beautiful and faithful testimonies. They are an inspirational family bringing Christ and Our Lady to the world. The *Betania* Foundation gives glory to God with the *Betania* Choir, directed by one of Maria Esperanza's daughters. They perform for all types of religious events all over Venezuela and wherever they are in the United States.

In 2015, they had prayed together as a family and felt God was telling them that *Señor* Geo and 36 other family members, including his daughters, husbands, son and his wife and many grandchildren plus *Betania* foundation members, should all come to OSMM. We hosted all of them for a week. You can imagine the quantity and variety of meals for that number of people aged from infancy to a senior citizen. The family believed they were always to be together in family units, so a hotel was out of the question. They stayed in all of our houses, plus the young men slept at our parish center, and all of their meals were served there.

We were privileged to again host the Bianchini family in October 2016, which was the last time they were able to travel to the United States as political tensions in Venezuela prevented travel. *Señor* Geo wanted to come to bless us and encourage us in our ministry even though he was quite ill at the time. He prayed for a special protection to surround and cover OSMM. He had become frail in the previous year and had difficulty walking and traveling. He spoke at the conference and gave many encouraging words to everyone. In December, we traveled to *Betania*, and *Señor* Geo was now on oxygen. Before we left for the airport to return home, he called us on the phone, telling us he would always remember us and said his last goodbye. On January 3, 2017, at age 90, *Señor* Geo was called from this world to the house of his Father. We desperately tried to go to his funeral, flying the first leg and waiting for our next flight. Everything that could go wrong did go wrong. Flights were canceled, and no amount of calling and pleading helped. After a whole day of travel, we had to fly back home without being able to leave the U.S. It was not in God's plan for us to attend his funeral.

During these years, we traveled twelve times to *Betania* to visit the Shrine and talk, pray and receive counsel from the family. We went to sit at the feet of *Señor* Geo as he would ask us questions and give us feedback about the direction we should go. He was the patriarch of the family, and he treated us as part of his family. He had a demeanor and a saintly look about him. His daughters, Maria Coromoto and Maria Grazie became our confidantes. They had a worldview of current events and events to come, and they gave us much advice on preparing for the future. We brought numerous people there for healing, prayer and pilgrimage. The word, *Betania,* means Bethany in Spanish, so we felt a special connection since our first home was called Bethany.

When travel became prohibitive, conditions in Venezuela deteriorated greatly. Food, fuel and medical supplies were scarce. It was a time of desperation for the country of Venezuela, including the Bianchini family. To help them with the essentials of food, personal supplies, medicine and other essentials, we began a donation drive. For six years, provisions were sent to Venezuela to help them survive. We raised the money, shipped the items to Miami in cargo containers, which continued on to Caracas, where the family was able to retrieve it. Literally, tens of thousands of dollars were raised each year in this mission. The family was sustained by this holy mission, and they were able to share much with the poor people who lived near their shrine. Supplies and food were given to a local seminary, for priests who could not get church supplies and for orphans at a local convent of religious sisters. Over a hundred water storage containers were sent to a leper colony operated by the Missionaries of Charity. One year, fifteen generators were shipped because the power was often shut off throughout the country. The Bianchini family saw to it that all the supplies and food went directly to those in need. Nothing was wasted or used for administrative purposes.

Over the last ten years or so, we have focused on healing and reconciliation. We have continued to have retreats that instruct and catechize people in the faith, but we see the greater need is for personal healing. Many people are carrying wounds from their childhood, their own bad decisions or circumstances in their lives. Their need to forgive

God, themselves and others is putting their spiritual growth and, in fact, even their salvation on hold. Whether it is the onslaught of the temptations of the flesh, the world or the devil, there is a great need for healing. Our retreats still focus on the Catholic faith and all it teaches, but we aim to help people heal of their own woundedness before they are able to love and follow Jesus and love themselves and others in a Christ-like way. Ultimately, our goal is to cooperate with God's grace to save souls.

After each retreat, we ask every priest who has spoken to OSMM, what their thoughts or sense of OSMM is and what we could do differently or better. They have helped us with their suggestions and consoled us with their compliments. With many of them speaking throughout the country, they bring a perspective that is invaluable to us.

In 2021, Fr. Seth Brown became the pastor of our parish and the chaplain of OSMM. He was an answer to our prayers. We had been praying for a chaplain who would step in with support and encouragement. He is truly a blessing and gift to us.

Everyone who attends our retreats is affected in a

unique way. Many people come in and instantly feel a peace about them. Almost everyone is in awe of beautiful statutory and liturgical items we have preserved. Over the years, we have noticed that people say they experience an overwhelming experience of the Holy Spirit when they enter the House of Bethany and especially when they come to the Sanctuary. They feel they are "coming home," safe, secure and at ease. They feel God. There is a sense of sacredness, beauty and truth here. We have filled the Sanctuary with holy objects, many of them from closed churches and even convents. These objects have been present for hundreds of prayers over decades of time. There is a history to all of it. More importantly, the many holy priests, speakers and saintly people who have walked on our grounds have brought so much with them. It is truly supernatural.

We have never felt it to the degree that others have experienced. We believe it is because our role is different from those who come here. We are being used to provide a place of sacredness where they can encounter God. It is almost as if a veil is in front of us, where we can see what others do, but we are not overwhelmed by it because it's our duty to maintain it for others.

Chapter 4

The People Within OSMM

From the beginning, people have come into our lives, some for a short while and others who have stayed on, but all of them have taught us something and led us on this journey. Whether they became a part of our ministry or were just here for a short time; some bit of wisdom is always left with us. Like Ecclesiastes, Chapter 3 tells us, "To every thing there is a season, and a time to every purpose under heaven." God has provided the people we needed to achieve His Divine Purpose all along the way.

As the ministry began, we had a number of people, some of whom were local friends and a few from around the area who helped out at our events. They worked with us for various lengths of time. The ministry had grown beyond what we had ever dreamed. We felt that some of the people who had been so involved with the ministry should be called formally to form a team and become part of OSMM. Everyone worked together to do whatever was needed to provide the retreats. After the first few years of thinking of our group as a team, Sr. Susan advised us, saying that we should not look at our group as a team but as a community. We were to be a group of people committed to one another and committed to spreading the love of Christ to everyone. The OSMM community was formed. We continued to ask people to join and help with the mission of the ministry. The ministry was expanding, and God provided by leading people to us who would support us and use their God-given talents. It was more than a group of like-minded people working together; it was like a family. There was an obvious love shared among the entire group. After long hours of working at a retreat, several of the community members would spend the night at our houses. Mary and Martha became the home for women, and the men stayed at the House of the Archangels. Late trips to Sonic Drive-in for ice cream and socializing became their routine. Returning to the houses, they would often stay up talking and sharing the faith. Some of the community looked forward to this as much as they did hosting the retreats.

The growth of the community coincided with the transition from conferences about the faith to helping people develop the skills to build a personal relationship with Jesus. We shifted from apologetics to prayer, healing and reconciliation. Prayer teams who prayed with retreatants during our retreats became an integral part of our ministry.

In addition to our Conference, Sr. Susan presented some community retreats, providing support and teaching for building our spiritual lives. We and the community members have grown in our own faith and spiritual lives through private retreats and the many gifted priests and speakers at our events. Sr. Susan told us that we were entrusted by God with a particular charism and were chosen to be the leaders of this ministry. We did not have any special skills, but God equipped us for what we needed to do. The community was formed to love, serve and be there for one another.

Mariann Timmermann
When we think of all the people who have been such an integral part of OSMM, we have to start with Mariann since she is the only one who has been with us the entire way from the very start. Many of you who are reading this will recognize Mariann as she is the one who greets you as you arrive at the registration desk. She has the gift of hospitality, able

to talk with all who enter and make them feel welcome. She has a smile and a kind word for everyone, knowing many of you by name as long-time friends.

When Mariann suffered serious health issues in 2013, we prayed and called every priest we knew to beg God for her healing. Thanks be to God, she is a survivor and continues to pour out her heart for the ministry.

For 25 years, Mariann has done countless and thankless jobs. She is a gardener, housekeeper, organizer, retreat mainstay and a helper in a myriad of ways. She does all the necessary but unglamourous jobs that go unnoticed by most, but we see the fruits of her labor. Mariann has traveled this long and, at times, difficult journey walking hand in hand with us, and we are forever and always grateful to her as she is a good and faithful servant of God.

John Seliga
We met John at the Fr. Rookey healing Masses in St. Louis. We became friends, and he became a great prayer warrior for us. John was there at the beginning of OSMM. He prepared us for what was to come. He

had the charism of hearing from God in his heart, and he would faithfully share his words with us. He led us, holding our hands and helping us to take the next step when we were so unsure and had so much to learn.

He was one of the leaders of our prayer teams, teaching by example and mentoring those who were new in the ministry. He was instrumental in OSMM obtaining The House of Bethany and the House of Mary and Martha. We probably would not have either house if it were not for his discernment and encouragement.

John was a loyal friend who was always there for us, supporting us personally and in the ministry. We could depend on him to drop everything and drive to Vandalia if we were in need. He leaves a hole that only he could fill.

Kathy Tuntland
Around 2006, a friend named Bill asked us to meet his good friend, Kathy, and her daughter Erin, who was troubled. We had to travel to north central Illinois to meet Kathy at her place of work along with

her husband and her daughter. We talked, asked questions and Kathy ended up bringing Erin to OSMM to meet with a priest for help. We developed a tight friendship, and Kathy felt compelled to become a part of OSMM. We felt like God had brought the three of us together. Kathy was a successful businesswoman and used her varied skills and talents for OSMM. She couldn't do enough for us and the ministry. She loved to be here and felt drawn to everything about OSMM. Her personality was all in, and she volunteered to do all she could. "If only I was closer, I would…." and she would list all the other types of tasks she could do.

She was alone in all of this as she sacrificed a lot to spend so much time and effort to support the ministry. She sacrificed by traveling over four hours to come here and by being away from her family, job and personal responsibilities.

Her daughter, Erin, developed a cancerous tumor in the middle of her liver, and it was considered inoperable. Lots of prayers were offered for Erin and Kathy. While we were in Lourdes on a pilgrimage, Kathy called us and told us that they had received the news that her daughter's tests had come back clear, and there was no indication of cancer. This was a true miracle as it was not medically possible. We were ecstatic.

Within a short time, Kathy developed ovarian cancer. She had been ill for a while but did not tell anyone. When she finally went to the doctor, her cancer had spread, and she was greatly suffering.

We went into action. Two trips were taken to seek healing. We traveled to Lourdes with Kathy. We took her to the healing baths and prayed for another miracle as her daughter had experienced. Kathy was receiving cancer treatments by now, but she bravely traveled on this trip, hoping for a cure. It was on this trip that we prayed at Fatima and received the confirmation that the Sanctuary should be built.

With great faith, we traveled with Kathy to Betania, Venezuela, to have our friends, the family of Servant of God Maria Esperanza, pray with her. We wanted to offer prayers at the apparition site where Our Lady had appeared many times over the years.

As the months went on, Kathy continued to worsen, and one particular time when we visited, we asked if she had offered her life for her daughter. She never answered directly but said, wouldn't any parent do the same?

Kathy was the major benefactor for the initial expense of building the Sanctuary. Her desire was to completely fund this endeavor for God, but it was not to pass. We went to visit her shortly before she passed away. All she wanted to talk about was the ministry. Though she was greatly suffering, she would not talk about herself. She kept telling us to grow and advance the ministry. She was courageous to the end.

She saw the Sanctuary in person one time, right after construction had begun. She was saddened by the fact that she would never see its completion. Kathy died on June 27, 2012, the feast of Our Lady of Perpetual Help.

Kathy Tuntland had traveled with us when we took Fr. Rookey on his last trip to the Holy Land. We had been there many times before, but this time, we noticed that wherever we went, we would see an image of Our Lady of Perpetual Help. We would see a painting on the wall or on an easel or even a statue. Our Lady was present throughout the pilgrimage.

Mary was speaking to us and Kathy on that trip, but we did not know what it meant. Only later did we see how Mary was already present and would soon accompany Kathy on the feast day of Our Lady of Perpetual Help to her eternal reward.

Anne Roberts

Anne Roberts began attending our retreats when she became aware of our ministry through a mailing. Somehow she quickly became part of our ministry.

She had many gifts that she readily shared with us. She was a big part of our prayer teams and mentored others on how to pray with people. Her ability to read into a person's heart and listen to the Holy Spirit soon became apparent to all who came to her for prayer. For a while, our prayer teams met with people in the living room of Bethany House during retreats. Long lines of people waited, sometimes for hours, to have Anne pray with them. She would speak to them from her heart, discerning what God wanted of them. It wasn't always easy to take that advice since her goal wasn't to console people but to lead them to a greater relationship with Jesus and Our Lady. That could translate into real change and work. When you spoke with Anne, she was focused on you. She was not distracted or inattentive. She treated everyone as if they were the most important person at that moment.

At retreats, Anne would sit in the back and take in all that was happening around us. At times, she advised us to pray for a particular intention or for protection. She was always in prayer even as she jumped in and helped with any job that needed to be done.

She became the person we went to for discernment for the ministry. As we have mentioned before, God always sends us people to help us find the path we should follow. Anne was that person in our personal lives and the ministry.

When Anne Roberts served as the leader of our prayer teams, she developed a one-of-a-kind relationship with Ann Stock. They formed a prayer team, and Anne R. truly loved and valued Ann. She spoke to us so many times about how much she loved Ann. It all came through praying together as a team. It was a special relationship formed through God.

When we called her, we were often met with her

gentle laugh as if she already knew what was on our minds. She didn't get upset when things went wrong; she would always first thank God for whatever circumstance had occurred. She truly believed in thanking God at all times, that He would bring good out of all things. If we had told Anne that our house had just burned down, her first words would have been, "Praise God." Anyone would think she was crazy or maybe had not heard correctly what was said. But Anne would insist that first, we praise God for all things, good or bad. We do not know God's purpose, but we know His plan is better than our plan.

If we thought something was hard or bad, she would gently correct us and remind us that we should see them as challenging, not bad. She didn't allow anyone to be down on themselves as that was rejecting who God has created you to be.

She deeply felt her faith at all times and in every circumstance. Anne became stricken with cancer, and by her attitude, you would not have known that. She received treatments at a hospital in St. Louis, and when the nurses would ask what she did for a living, she would reply, "I'm a missionary." Of course, their next question was, "Where?" She would answer,

"Right here." She truly was a missionary as she would talk and pray with those around her receiving treatments and the staff about Jesus and her faith.

When she knew she wasn't going to recover, we were devastated, but Anne was at peace. She told us that it is a win-win. "If I get better, I'll still be here. If I die, I will go to heaven." We don't know anyone who had faith like hers.

Once when she was hospitalized, one of her roommates came to greatly know Jesus through Anne's courage and attitude facing her illness, and they became friends. She was in great pain and suffering but still kept thinking of others first.

Fr. Ermelindo, who had brought us the relics of Padre Pio, offered Mass at her house as we gathered around her dining room table. When Fr. Seraphim Michalenko MIC, was going back to the airport, we stopped with him to celebrate Mass there again. You may recognize Fr. Seraphim as one of the translators of Sr. Faustina's Diary of Divine Mercy.

During her final few months, we would visit her at her home and try to absorb as much as we could from her speaking to us about the ministry. We would take notes and even try to tape her words on our phones. We hung on her every word and hated to leave her each time.

She was visited by many priests and received the anointing of the sick, confession, and Holy Communion. She guarded her every word, never wanting to commit a single sin as she so desired to go to heaven.

There were hundreds of friends and priests who prayed for Anne as she was loved by so many people. Her dining room was filled with mass cards and get-well cards. But, God's plans were not ours. Sadly, Anne passed away on May 11, 2013, and we miss her dearly. When she died, we felt like a part of our hearts died with her.

She was faithful to OSMM to a fault. For a couple of years, we wore blue shirts for our retreats. Anne would talk to all of the community members about the privilege we had serving God through OSMM. Sometimes, people were tempted to go their own way, but Anne admonished them, saying "Never give up your blue shirt". She knew the power of personal protection from belonging to a ministry led by God and Our Lady and she didn't want anyone to wander away from that. Her laugh, her demeanor and her words are deeply missed and she is never far from our thoughts.

Ann Stock
Ann joined the ministry full-time in 2009. She had helped out during our first few years by working with St. Joseph Communications, who recorded our events and sold their own merchandise. She helps manage our store, updates our website, sends out our email campaigns and helps with the maintenance of our buildings. We count on her each and every day for many things, but most of all for her friendship, faithfulness and encouragement. She is our rock and our fortress to calm the storms inside and outside of OSMM.

Mary Adams
We knew Mary as a parishioner at Mother of Dolors. She is a hard-working, dependable woman and extremely loyal. She was diagnosed with lymphoma in 2007 and, having beaten it once, faced another bout two years later. She underwent a bone marrow transplant and was obviously very sick and suffering. Our good friend and community member, Sara, worked at Barnes Hospital in St. Louis, where Mary was receiving treatment. We called on Sara often to

pray for those we knew in the hospital since she is a physician's assistant and a powerful prayer warrior. Sara was an integral part of our prayer teams for many years. We asked Sara to look up Mary and pray with her. Sara devotedly visited Mary throughout her hospital stay, and Mary could depend on her for support. Thanks be to God, Mary recovered and soon became a part of the ministry. She helped in a myriad of ways and became a part of our prayer teams, primarily with Ann Stock. Mary continues to support us by sending out prayer requests for our community.

Annie Karto
Annie is Catholic singer who brought her beautiful voice to Our Sorrowful Mother's Ministry early on. She sang at all of our conferences and retreats. She accompanied us on several pilgrimages, singing at Masses and in the evenings. Her songs are so heartfelt, and her voice so beautiful. She has such a heart for God.

Annie wrote this song specifically for OSMM. We felt it really hit the mark, describing our personal struggles and our faith journey.

Come to the Cross

Come to the Cross, Come stand by me
I, who am your Mother, Love you tenderly
I see your tears, I know your pain
In my pierced heart, I've felt the same

Sorrowful Mother
when you take away my fears
My concerns for my family
Heartaches of these years
Sometimes I want to turn away
Then I hear you gently say

Come to the Cross, Come stand by me
I, who am your Mother, Love you tenderly
I see your tears, I know your pain
In my pierced heart, I've felt the same

Sorrowful Mother,
When you take me by the hand
Give me courage and wisdom
To grow and understand
This journey of love requires one thing
I surrender my life and so I sing

I'll come to the cross, I'll stand by you
I, who am your child, tenderly love you too.

I'll dry your tears, I share your pain.
Then my own heart I'll feel the same

Come to the Cross

Matthew Baute
We became acquainted with Matthew Baute through Annie Karto. He lived in St. Louis, and he would come to the retreats and play the piano while Annie sang. He became a large part of our ministry for several years, bringing love, joy and faith through his music ministry. He met the love of his life, Leah, through OSMM, and together they have formed a beautiful Christ-filled family with their children. Though moving to be closer to extended family, they still are a part of OSMM with their love and prayers. We are grateful to Matthew for his faithfulness and his friendship.

Our Family of Community Members
From our very first event, there have been people who have helped us in many ways. We would ask local people and friends to help set up and tear down for retreats. There was always a lot of moving of podiums, tables, displays and banners. People have come and gone over the years. When we formalized

our community, we also enlisted people who may not be able to be here physically but are our prayer warriors. We have grown to about thirty-five members at this time, and they fill various needs for us. Patty is here every retreat to provide meals for our speakers. Barb is here to do basically any job we throw at her. Joan comes and spends days cleaning the houses and sanctuary. Deborah came and started her own Pro-Life apostolate. For many years, Ted and Randy came and worked physically and financially to provide whatever we asked for the ministry.

Over twenty-five years, the number of people who have given of themselves for this ministry is what has enabled us to grow and continue. There are so many who go unnamed, but we are eternally grateful for their support of OSMM.

We are also grateful for the many people who have supported OSMM financially. Ministry may be a work of God, but it nonetheless takes money to run. There are mortgages, utilities, constant repairs and upkeep just like everyone faces. We are so thankful for the monthly donors who have supported us, several of them for many years. Whenever there is a need, God has provided generous hearts who have come forward and provided. We are constantly amazed at how Our Lord and Our Lady have carried us through the hardest times.

In short, all of you who have given so much for OSMM know who you are. More importantly, the Lord knows your heart and your generosity. By living a life of the Beatitudes, your reward will be heaven. We often joke about how joyous it will be when we reach heaven and see all the people who have impacted our lives and those whose lives were impacted by OSMM.

Chapter 5

We Share in the Sorrows with Our Sorrowful Mother

In the 25 years since we began, there have inevitably been sorrows along the way. We have walked together with several community members during serious illnesses in which God granted them the healing they desired. In addition to Kathy Tuntland and Anne Roberts, we have lost several of our community members, and we want to honor their memory and their lives.

Sue Young
We came to know Sue through the same priest who advised us to have smaller monthly retreats. In 2005, Vanessa was going through a life crisis, and we were advised to go see Sue, who lived in Louisville, KY. Fr. Crotty said she was a mystic and strong prayer warrior.

We drove through an ice storm to get there, but it was worth every harrowing minute.
Sue led the Marian Center there and had a prayer

group. When we arrived, Father was there, and he and Sue began praying with Vanessa. It was an experience we will never forget. She knew everything about Vanessa's life and what she was enduring, though no one had told her. The entire room of her prayer group was praying and crying, and she was completely stunned. It changed her life forever, and Sue became our trusted mentor and friend from that day forward.

Sue helped guide us through many highs and lows over the years. We saw her regularly in Louisville, and she also came to Vandalia for the retreats and to mentor the OSMM community. Sue was unlike anyone we have known and had many gifts of mysticism, and was truly connected to God. Sue told us we do not have the luxury of treating the ministry as "just one of things we do." The ministry is not something we do; it is who we are. Over the years, we depended on Sue for prayer and advice. When she became ill with cancer, she moved to Florida to be near her daughter. After several years of suffering, Sue died peacefully on October 30, 2021. May she rest in peace.

Chris Mars

Chris was a community member who had a heart of gold. She was the type of person who would do anything for anyone. She was always full of joy and enthusiasm, never complaining, just going about her business, working hard. She became the cook for OSMM as, for a few years, we offered meals at retreats. Chris could take the simplest meal and make it into something fit for a king. She had the ability to prepare meals for large groups of people single-handedly and loved every minute of it.

Chris was like a sponge absorbing all the talks from our speakers. She loved to learn more about being a Catholic and a woman of God and grew deeply in her faith.

Very unexpectedly, Chris passed away suddenly from a heart attack. Our hearts broke when her family called to share the tragic news. We were in shock that she was taken without warning on September 2, 2012, at age 53. In front of the Sanctuary, there is a large statue of an angel weeping over a pillar. It is dedicated to our friend, Chris. The plaque asks all who pass by to offer a prayer for this beautiful soul.

John Frailey

John was one of our early community members who served as a Knight. The Knights were a group of men that served the ministry for a few years. They could be depended upon to help with retreats and do anything asked of them. Even with a wife and growing family of eight children, John helped whenever he could. Sadly, he was stricken with leukemia, and with the bravest fight we have ever witnessed, he passed away on December 15, 2013. There is a statue of the Sacred Heart of Jesus in front of the Sanctuary dedicated to John.

Bob Frey

The best way to describe Bob is that he was a gentle, holy soul. He had an uncanny resemblance to Blessed Solanus Casey and exemplified many of the same virtues. He came to our retreats with his wife, Jody, and they quickly became community members and helped in many ways. Bob was always joyful, kind and had a heart full of love for everyone. He became a cherished member of our prayer teams.

Bob was a gifted woodworker and made many of the plaques and cases that house our relics. Whenever we look at the many items he crafted and donated to us, we recall his quiet demeanor, boyish smile and humble heart. Bob passed away on December 26, 2019. There is a small tribute to Bob in the prayer room he used to help others.

Carolyn Ewen
Carolyn was a giving and holy soul. She always arrived at the retreats with the best cookies and treats we have ever had. She was very generous and loved the Church. She entered eternity on August 2, 2013.

Chapter 6

Building the Dream

House of Bethany

The House of Bethany is a place of refuge that is reserved for clergy. It is located directly across the street from our parish, Mother of Dolors Catholic Church. This home was owned by a local couple since the 1990s. It came on the market in 2004 and seemed perfect for the ministry as we felt that a permanent place for OSMM was needed. With only $500 for a down payment, we needed a miracle. John Seliga called us to say we should give earnest money to the realtor for the purchase of the house. We took his advice in this huge leap of faith. That evening we buried Miraculous Medals all around a large Blue Spruce in the front yard of the house and prayed for a miracle. On Sunday, Debbie decided to call a friend to ask her for prayers for another concern. She did not usually call people on Sundays but felt she would this time. When her friend answered, she seemed a little surprised and said she wanted to put her husband on the line. This was odd as we had only met the husband once. Quite to our astonishment, the friend's husband told her that he had been thinking about donating the money for Debbie to purchase Bethany House. He had told his wife that he would donate it if Debbie would call that day. God's plan worked perfectly. On the feast day of Our Lady of LaSalette and St. Januarius, September 19, 2004, the funds to purchase Bethany House were donated. We made another night visit to the house to dance around the spruce tree with great joy and to thank Our Lady for her help!

This home designated for priests would become a big part of OSMM. Interestingly enough, this house was Debbie's childhood home. She lived there during her childhood and teen years. Her parents had moved a few years previously.

Soon after, John Seliga and two of his friends from St. Louis visited the newly purchased house. They went down to the basement while we remained upstairs. We heard beautiful singing coming from the basement. When John and his friends came upstairs, they remarked that they too heard angels singing. There was no other explanation for the beautiful singing as we had both heard it independently. Bethany was truly a miracle.

By 2006, we were able to convert the basement level into a chapel. Though it was not requested, a letter from Bishop George Lucas, at the time the Bishop of the Diocese of Springfield, arrived on September 15, the Feast of Our Lady of Sorrows. It granted permission to OSMM to repose the Blessed Sacrament in the chapel, called Mary's Chapel. We called Sr. Susan in tears, wondering what this meant that the Bishop was bestowing this great honor of allowing us to have the Blessed Sacrament permanently present in our chapel, and we had not even requested it. She told us that this just doesn't happen. But God had other plans, and the chapel has been used for adoration, prayer, Holy Mass and private meditation.

The House of Bethany is a place of peaceful prayer for visiting priests, religious and the OSMM community members. It is available free of charge for priests to come and rest.

The grounds of Bethany House include the 14 Stations of the Cross, 7 Stations of Our Lady of Sorrows, a reflecting pool with seating, a St. Francis Garden, a shrine to Our Lady, Reconciler of All

People and Nations, and beautiful rose and floral gardens. It is truly a place of peace and beauty of God's creation.

House of Mary and Martha

Our friend, Kathy Tuntland, had a friend who dreamt that Kathy was to buy a house on a hill with water running near it. The dream occurred on Monday, March 19, 2007, the feast day of St. Joseph, but the feast day didn't mean anything to the friend as she was a Baptist.

During a retreat weekend before the dream, John Seliga and another community member had gone into the backyard of the House of Bethany because we were trying to decide what to do with the garage. We were considering making the garage into living space and completing some much-needed landscaping. We tried to force a rod into the ground and to find water as John's friend Annette had drawn a picture of the pool of Bethesda and associated it with the house. Annette was able to describe the pool, its depth and the rocks surrounding it. That night the readings were from John 5: 7-8 *The sick man answered him, "Sir, I have no one to put me into the pool when the water is stirred up; while I am on my way, someone else gets down there before me." Jesus said to him, "Rise, take up your mat, and walk."* and Ezekiel, Chapter 47: *Then he brought me back to the entrance of the temple, and there! I saw water flowing out from under the threshold of the temple toward the east, for the front of the temple faced east. The water flowed out toward the right side of the temple to the south of the altar.*

John announced we needed to buy the house across the alley. He felt like he was swept across the lawn and into the yard of the home. We were certainly not ready for this as we had just acquired Bethany, and this was not even a consideration. This was besides the fact that the house was not for sale. Somehow, we trusted that this must be part of God's plan and didn't question where this was heading.

Strangely enough about this time, Debbie was walking near the house, and out of the blue, the owner shouted out the window that Debbie should buy her house. After all this came to pass, Kathy decided to purchase the house. The house was in disrepair and needed many renovations.

Kathy also envisioned an outdoor building designed to represent the Holy Sepulcher where Christ was buried. We purchased a small building, and within it is a lifesize statue of Christ lying in repose with the interior textured with stucco to resemble the interior of a stone tomb. When our painter, Chris D. was working inside the building that we commonly refer to as the tomb, she noticed an image of a dove in the ceiling that is formed in the plaster. She asked if it was there by design. It may be, but it was not our design but Divine Providence. Visitors can clearly see the image when they look up at the ceiling near the statue of Christ. The Holy Sepulcher has a small tabernacle which is dedicated to Kathy that is used during retreats. It is a beautiful, holy place to pray.

House of the Archangels
In 2008, a third home was purchased and donated to OSMM. It was called the House of the Archangels and was dedicated to Saint Michael, St. Raphael and St. Gabriel. The three large statues of the Archangels we had received from Holy Angels Church several years previously were the namesake for this house and were present in the main living area.

The house also served as a museum-like setting for all of the personal items of Fr. Tom McCarthy and Fr. Peter Rookey. Many of the possessions and artifacts of their respective ministries were displayed in the home. In 2009, the front portion of the house was converted into a chapel dedicated to Our Sorrowful Mother, appropriately called *Stabat Mater*. It contained the large Pieta statue we now have in the Sanctuary. The upstairs of the home was used for members of OSMM to stay during retreats. It became a home of great camaraderie and friendship. The home served its purpose for several years, but the site was meant for greater things.

Sanctuary of the Sorrowful Mother
As the ministry grew, so did the large number of supplies needed to hold our events. From setting up tables, displaying books and sacramentals to sell and then tearing it all down and packing it away until the next month, it had become harder and harder to move all the artifacts needed to put on our events each month. This was in addition to podiums, statues, and liturgical items for Mass, confession and adoration. For a long time, we also had meals available during retreats. About the same time, we began to experience scheduling conflicts with the different venues we were using. It seemed like blocks were popping up regularly and causing us interference in hosting our events.

Some community members who we depended on for prayer began to tell us that we needed our own building. They felt that God was calling us to do so. Since some key people in the ministry felt that we were supposed to build our own chapel, we were praying throughout a pilgrimage we took in 2011 as to where God was leading us. This would be a great leap of faith to take on such a huge financial investment, and we did not take it lightly. While we were in Fatima with our dear friend, Anne Roberts, she told us that she received in prayer that we were to build our own chapel. Anne's discernment was the final confirmation we needed to construct our own building.

Brainstorming began. Where would we build? How would we pay for it? What should it look like? In order to keep in proximity to our other two houses, we decided that we would look at the lot behind the House of the Archangels. We quickly deduced that the space was too small. We made the very hard decision to tear down the House of the Archangels and build on that site.

Building plans were drawn up, literally on scraps of

paper. We know that no one takes on a project like this without an architect's drawings and certified blueprints. But, we didn't operate that way. We had an architect's rough drawing of the exterior of the building, but that was all. We began to plan out the interior space. We needed a large main room for Mass and the conferences by the speakers. We also knew we needed space for prayer rooms, a space to display and sell our religious items, a small kitchen and other essentials like restrooms, a utility room, etc.

We buried medals in the foundation, and Msgr. Swetland blessed all of the property. We talked to Kathy about many of the details of the actual building and how she envisioned the layout. After taking out a construction loan to cover the actual building of the Sanctuary, it was understood that Kathy would be able to pay off the mortgage. As Kathy continued to suffer from her illness, she thought it was all arranged. Kathy passed away with no paperwork finalized, the building was completed, and we faced the huge liability of paying for the building. As we prepared to furnish the interior, we had to seek donors for everything. All of the interior was obtained piecemeal by seeking donors for each and every item.

Our first event in the new building was on April 13, 2012, with Fr. Martin-Edward Ohajunwa. On June 24, Bishop Thomas John Paprocki dedicated and consecrated the new building. He personally came up with the name, "The Sanctuary of the Sorrowful Mother." When he suggested it to us, we knew that was what it would be called. Prior to this, we had come up with some other suggestions. One that was most likely to have been chosen was the Refuge of the Remnant. We saw ourselves as one of those groups who would persevere until the end, no matter how hard things would become in the future. So, in a way, that title is still part of us as we have been told by several different people that this will be a place people will come to when the world gets more difficult to live in as a Christian.

Ave Maria House
Another property we had for a while was a little house a few blocks Northeast of the Sanctuary. We became aware of it because it was nearby and was available for a bargain price. We didn't need to do very much to it, except furnish it and, of course, equip it with religious statues and sacramentals. It served for a few years as a place for visiting OSMM members to stay when they were in town for events,

and many of our speakers stayed there too. After a few years, a friend who had been to a few retreats expressed her desire to move to Vandalia and become an OSMM member. We were able to sell her the house, and she has been a prayer warrior for the ministry ever since.

House of Mary, Reconciler of All People and Nations

Soon after building the Sanctuary, the neighbors to the South of our property began to entertain the thought of selling their homes to us. We were not looking to buy more property, but the opportunity to have the west side and south ends of the block were too good to be true. In fact, it wasn't just an opportunity; it was God placing before us what we needed to do. We purchased the house directly south of the Sanctuary and dedicated it to Our Lady as she appeared in *Betania*, Venezuela: Mary, Reconciler of All People and Nations.

Little Lambs Christian Day Care

Directly adjacent to the south of Mary, Reconciler of All People/Nations house was an empty lot. It was owned by a family whose home is on the east side of the lot. The interesting thing about this empty lot is that it was the location of the original Catholic Church rectory. The adjacent church existed in the mid-1850s until the late 1890s, when it burned to the ground, and the decision was made to move the parish approximately one block to the northeast, where it stands today. Little Lambs stands on the hallowed ground where the church had stood. When the family who owned this property approached us to purchase their home, we prayed about it and knew what we needed to do. We have always had a deep devotion to children, and Debbie's daughter also had the dream of one day operating a daycare. This was the purpose of this property. Renovations and remodeling to meet state standards and accommodate the space for little ones began. It has become a very successful and much-needed childcare facility for our town, with Debbie's daughter taking over ownership of the property and business.

House of the Immaculate Conception
The corner house to the north of the Sanctuary was landlocked with the Sanctuary to its south and the House of Mary and Martha to its east. We always felt we were supposed to own this property and many people confirmed this to us. In late 2021, we prayed a novena to Our Lady of the Immaculate Conception,

and on the Solemnity of the Immaculate Conception (December 8), we received a notice that the people who owned this house would sell it to us. They had never shown any interest in this before. So in early 2022, we closed on the property and began major renovations. No updates had been done in this home for many years. Exterior siding, painting, new windows and doors, landscaping, interior painting, drywalling, and renovating the bathroom and kitchen were all very much needed. The original oak floors were stripped and looked like new.

We did not plan to renovate the lower level, but when Bishop Paprocki gave us permission to have another chapel with the Blessed Sacrament, we were thrilled. Work continues on this new chapel dedicated to St. Joseph with pews, altar, tabernacle and many other items all obtained from closed churches. These beautiful items have been restored and now will be returned to their former purpose for the Glory of God.

Chapter 7

Priests/Speakers

Karl Keating
We hosted Karl Keating of Catholic Answers at one of our early conferences. We told him we had no assets and just paid for things by making a plea for donations, and the money would come in. He told us that no one does that!

Fr. Bill Casey CPM
Fr. Bill Casey has been a dear and beloved friend for 25 years. We are thankful for his leadership, encouragement and support. Fr. Casey has been loyal to us to a fault, no matter what our need. He makes himself available for us when we have questions or just need his words of support. Even with his demanding schedule as a Father of Mercy giving conferences and parish missions throughout the U.S, he has served as our Retreat Master for the Annual Conference at least ten times. We continue to call on him as the people look forward to his powerful and faith-filled talks. We are grateful for God placing him in our lives. The Fathers of Mercy have presented

many times over the years, and they are a mainstay of our retreats.

Bishop Thomas John Paprocki
Bishop Paprocki became the Bishop of the Diocese of Springfield in Illinois in 2010. He has been a supporter of OSMM and has spoken here several times at our Annual Conference. In June of 2012, he came to celebrate Mass and consecrate our altar. He is generous with his time, and we value his advice when he visits. We admire his strong, orthodox leadership and are grateful for his continued support.

In August of 2012, we were contacted by the bishop's office to come to Springfield for a meeting. We are committed to following the magisterium of the Church in all manners, so we wondered what this meeting was concerning. Bishop Paprocki greeted us with wonderful news; he had named OSMM a Private Association of the Faithful on August 15, 2012, the Solemnity of the Assumption of Mary. We were thrilled about this official proclamation and affirmation of the ministry.

We are grateful to him for continuing to allow us to have the Blessed Sacrament in Mary's Chapel at

Bethany and the Stabat Mater Dolorosa Chapel in the Sanctuary. We are thankful for his permission to have the Blessed Sacrament in the new Chapel of St. Joseph in the House of the Immaculate.

Fr. Ermelindo Di Capua, OFM Cap
We had heard about the relics of Padre Pio traveling through the United States. We knew we had to have them here for people to pray with and venerate. Contacting the Shrine at San Giovanni Rotundo, we were able to set it up. A Capuchin priest named Fr. Ermelindo traveled to America with two relics; a cloth containing blood from the stigmata along with one of the gloves worn by Padre Pio were displayed. He had been in Pietrelcina at the same time as Padre Pio and learned English so he would be able to respond to the thousands of letters Padre Pio received on a regular basis. He was the head of the English Office there for many years. He was a humble man who loved to tell of Padre Pio's holiness and tell many personal stories of the many mystical gifts of this great saint. We loved his quiet manner and how he started his talks with the word, "generally" before he would explain some happenstance with Padre Pio. We had him bring the relics a second time, and he stayed with us several

days. A great gift to us was he brought along a First Class Relic of Padre Pio and presented it to OSMM. It is a piece of cloth with Padre Pio's blood.

Though he was in his eighties, he wanted to make good use of his time here, so we took him for a boat ride on Vandalia Lake and then to St. Louis, where he went up to the top of the Gateway Arch to view the city. He traveled alone and said he was never worried about flight arrangements or anything else because he had his friend Padre Pio with him all the time.

Fr. Andrew Apostoli, CFR
Fr. Andrew was one of the founding members of the Franciscan Friars of the Renewal in the New York area. He and Fr. Benedict Groeschel, along with others, formed the order to return to basics and center their ministry on the poor. Fr. Andrew lived simply without many modern conveniences we take for granted and worked helping the poor, drug addicts and others abandoned by society. He was a talented author and teacher who appeared regularly on EWTN.

He became a dear friend; kind, gentle, humble and

always joyful, taking time to advise us and teach us. He loved people and loved to come and present retreats for us, always taking time to answer questions and explain the answers. He authored numerous books, among them *Fatima for Today*. Our Lord blessed him by allowing him to live through 2017, the 100th anniversary of the apparitions at Fatima, and he died peacefully on December 13, 2017.

We recall a story from when we picked up Fr. Andrew and a couple of the Religious Sisters from his order at the airport. Thinking they would like to go somewhere special for dinner since they live such a simple life, we took them to Lombardo's, a fine Italian restaurant well known in St. Louis. They ordered fried fish and French fries! They said they never got to eat that kind of food, so it was a treat for them.

John LaBriola
We became aware of the powerful work John was doing in teaching people about spiritual warfare and giving them real-life ways to combat it. We hosted him for the first time in 2009. He has been a great friend and our supporter. He is someone we can turn to for discernment and encouragement because he

has a personal and deep understanding of God's call for OSMM. John tells it straight with no fluff. His discernment is exact and true. He is a valuable ally when circumstances are challenging. We have been privileged to have him return several times to present retreats and pray with us for the ministry.

Fr. Chad Ripperger
For several years, we attended the Healing and Deliverance Conference at the University of St. Mary of the Lake, Mundelein Seminary. This conference is restricted to priests and a few lay people who are involved in healing ministry. With a recommendation from our bishop, we were able to attend for several years. In 2013, Fr. Chad Ripperger was the keynote speaker. We were immediately impressed with his vast knowledge of deliverance and spiritual warfare; we knew we wanted to get to know him better. He is considered one of the premier experts in this field of ministry. We really wanted him to come to OSMM and present retreats for us, and we relished the thought of him teaching and training us in ways we could help others. Having him come to OSMM and meet with a couple of laywomen was as likely as us winning the lottery. We wrote a note to Fr. Ripperger with our information

and gave it to Margarett, who was hosting the conference, to pass on to him along with Margarett's recommendation. Amazingly, he gave us his phone number. With much persistence, he agreed, and we couldn't believe it.

In 2014, Fr. Ripperger, along with Dr. Margarett Schlientz, who was one of the organizers of the Mundelein conference, came and presented a weekend retreat. The following year, he presented three separate weekend retreats.

In 2016, Father very generously came to present four retreats. On one weekend, Fr. Daniel McElheron, one of his fellow priests in the Doloran Fathers, accompanied him. He came another weekend to train all of the OSMM members on how to pray effectively with people and how to recognize and combat spiritual attacks.

In 2017, Fr. Ripperger presented one retreat and has since stopped almost all public appearances, except for coming here to OSMM. His primary focus is establishing the Society of the Most Sorrowful Mother, the "Doloran Fathers," who work in cooperation with the local bishop to provide assistance to those in the most spiritual need. The

Doloran Fathers are a semi-contemplative order, so they spend several hours a day in prayer.

He is currently in the Archdiocese of Denver working with those afflicted spiritually and continues to write books. Because of our friendship with him, he recently presented a couple of conferences for us in order to lend his support for OSMM.

It has been such an honor for us that Fr. Ripperger, who is so highly sought after for conferences, would take time to teach us and present at conferences. He has become for us a spiritual father. We ask him for advice and he guides us so we always stay within the teachings of the Church and within our own authority as lay people. He has filled the hole that was left since Fr. Rookey has passed away. As usual, God provided us with the person we needed to keep the ministry on track. We are blessed to have Fr. Ripperger as our friend, mentor and advisor.

Chapter 8

Preserving the Sacred

Windows and Religious Items

Many people who come to OSMM ask us where we acquired the many altars, statues and liturgical appointments in our Sanctuary. All of them have a story, and we have a small tour book we use to walk the grounds and tell the stories.

One of the most beautiful and large windows we have is directly above our altar in the Sanctuary. It is nine feet tall and eight feet wide. It depicts Christ lovingly embracing His Mother. In the background, four apostles sit and wait for Him. This window is a representation of a painting by Bernhard Plockhorst called, "Jesus Taking Leave of His Mother." The depth of the images of this window changes as the sun moves during the day. Different flowers and plants, the sky and even buildings in the background become more visible. This window was covered up by paneling in a church and was discovered during some renovations. Incredibly, the parish did not want to keep this window, and we jumped at the chance to own it and give it new life.

The window that adorns the front of the Sanctuary is called "Jesus and Mary" and was painted by Carl Shoenherr (1824-1906) and is eight feet tall and ten feet wide. It shows Jesus immediately after the Resurrection with Mary Magdalene kneeling before him. "Touch me not, for I am not yet ascended to my Father. " John 20:17

On the wall separating the foyer from the main sanctuary are two windows representing the Annunciation. The Holy Spirit is shown on one window, and Mary is on the other window. What many people do not know is that this was originally one window. In order to work around the main doors entering the sanctuary, the window was altered. It was craftily split in half, and the outside border was duplicated to surround each window. It was so expertly done that there is no way to distinguish the original border from the new.

Within the Sanctuary, we have a stained glass window that is framed and backlit. It depicts a painting from 1888 by Heinrich Hofmann called

"Jesus at the Home of Mary and Martha at Bethany." We have a personal devotion to Mary and Martha, so this was an important window for us to display right outside the Blessed Sacrament Chapel in the Sanctuary.

Just outside the door of the Stabat Mater Dolorosa Chapel is a statue of Jesus at Gethsemane. He is being comforted by an angel as He is overcome in His Agony. It was created by a famous religious artist from St. Louis named Max Schneiderhahn in 1903. The statue had been removed from a church and was being stored in a basement closet. We were at the church to go to confession and saw it in a closet with the angel's wing sticking out. We went home and called the pastor to see if we could buy it, and he was glad to sell it to us.

The main altar used in the Sanctuary was acquired from a convent established by Mother Cabrini for the Missionary Sisters of the Sacred Heart. It is constructed with wood but is inlaid with mosaic tiles and has four marble pillars supporting the altar along the length of its front side.

Not many people can say they have seen a statue like

the St. Michael the Archangel that we have on display. We always admired this commanding sculpture when we visited a close friend and benefactor of OSMM, who had this statue at his place of business. One day, out of the blue, he asked if we wanted it. Of course, we said yes! The statue is approximately six-and-a- half feet tall, his wingspan is six feet wide and weighs well over 100 lbs. St. Michael sits atop a former side altar and reaches out near the ceiling to wield his sword over the evil one. St. Michael is one of our favorite saints, as there are at least three other statues of him in the sanctuary.

One of the rare statues we have is a near life-size depiction of the Dying St. Joseph, held by the figures of Jesus and Mary. People may not realize that St. Joseph is the patron of those near death, as he must have died in the most perfect way in the arms of Our Lord and Our Lady.

One of the most striking statues we have is of the Scourged Christ. It is nearly four feet tall, and the artist created it to present Christ as he would have truly looked after being brutally scourged with whips. The skin is torn, and muscle is exposed, showing what would have resulted from the scourging. It is disturbing to look at and meditate on, and that is the point of it. Artwork generally shows a small cut on the side and maybe a few minor marks. Our Lord suffered tremendously, and this statue represents the true image.

We have large statues of St. John the Baptist, St. Benedict, Mother Teresa, St. Maximilian Kolbe, Padre Pio, Our Lady of Mt. Carmel, the Pieta and many images of Mary as she appeared at Fatima, LaSalette, Guadalupe and Lourdes. Needless to say, we have several depictions of Jesus and Mary, especially Our Lady in her Sorrows.

There are countless stories that go along with the many statues, pieces of artwork, relics and church furnishings we have been able to have for OSMM. We have described some of them above, but space and time don't allow for all of them to be described. We love to take people on tours of our place and explain the stories to them. We have compiled a booklet to try and preserve all of the details.

Chapter 9

Pilgrimages

We began our pilgrimages as a fundraiser for OSMM and to deepen our spiritual lives. We visited numerous holy places every year, sometimes taking two or three pilgrimages within a year's time. We had many holy priests lead these encounters for us, and each one brought their own gifts to our journey. They were a gift for many who traveled with us. We didn't benefit financially, but the grace we received praying in these holy places was priceless. It was our joy to watch those we invited to experience the peace and love we first felt when we saw the places Jesus walked and the saints lived.

One of the graces of visiting the Holy Land is the experience of being where Christ lived, taught, suffered and redeemed us. The faith became more alive when we touched the spot where the cross stood; knelt and prayed over the stone where Mary held the dead body of Jesus, and stood in the tomb where Jesus lay. Everything in the Holy Land was incredible and life-changing when you let the reality of what happened there sink in. The Gospel readings, especially during Advent and Lent, are like an open picture in your mind when you recall walking on that same ground and stones and touching the waters of the Jordan River and the Sea of Galilee. They have truly enriched our lives.

The pilgrimages to Italy are second only to the Holy Land. It is the center of our faith with St. Peter's, the Vatican, all of the major basilicas and churches, and the catacombs. Even with our many trips there, it is impossible to visit all the significant religious and historical places in Rome. We were able to visit Assisi, Siena, Loreto, San Giovanni Rotunda, Lanciano and many other sites of Eucharistic Miracles.

Msgr. Swetland was the spiritual leader of many of our early pilgrimages. His vast knowledge of the faith and the places we visited made all of these trips a tremendous learning experience. He used them to help form us in our faith and advise us. We not only learned about growing the ministry, but he advised us on everything from logistics of running the ministry to our own spiritual growth. Once when we were at St. Peter's Basilica in Rome, he gave us the advice to stand on our own and not to depend on any other entity to support us. We have followed that model supporting the ministry entirely through donations from individuals. It's a grassroots endeavor financed through the generosity of people.

One thing that surprised us as Americans is how different we are from Europeans in social ways. When you travel outside the U.S., you soon find out Americans are basically the only people who wait in lines, observe signage, especially traffic signs and follow directions. As Americans, we like order and fairness, so when it was time for communion at Mass, we would walk up row by row and return orderly back to our own seats. This was not the case in Italy and even some other countries. A few minutes before Communion, people would start getting up and moving around. A person from the back may walk all the way up to the front and wait. It was not uncommon to have some jostling for position or even an elbow thrown. Even after the lines would start to form at Communion, it was not uncommon for someone from across the church to walk up the line, mumble a "*scusi*" and get in line in front of you or wherever they chose.

There are numerous concrete posts along the curbs in

many foreign countries to prevent people from parking on the sidewalks, sideways or pretty much anywhere their car will fit. Keeping groups together and on time was a continuous challenge. There are always a few who need to take that "one" extra picture or buy one more souvenir. We have never lost anyone on any of our trips, but every pilgrimage had its challenges and most times, humorous ones.

When we were in Venezuela, we attended Mass in Caracas and expected it to be just like America. We arrived 15 minutes early and took our seats. There were lots of people in front of the church talking and visiting before Mass. A few people came in, but some went back out. This continued for a short while. Even the priest was outside for a while and then came in. We stood up, thinking Mass was starting since it was the time it should have begun. But no, he just went up front to do something and then went back out for a few minutes, so we sat back down. Eventually, there was a procession, so we discovered Mass begins when the priest decides to begin.

During the Mass, it was not unusual for toddlers or small children to wander around, even walk up toward the altar and sit down. Their parents didn't seem to mind; it was just accepted that kids do that. Of course, in America, we whisk our kids to the cry room at the first outburst, but the Venezuelan people were more relaxed, and no one seemed to care.

In Fatima, Portugal, we were able to see the homes of the seers, their childhood parish, the apparition site and, of course, the Basilica of Our Lady of the Rosary. While at Fatima, we were walking past the Holm Oak tree where our Lady appeared to the children. It is a rather large tree with a raised wall and fence around it to keep people back. It is not positive that this is the original tree since soon after the apparitions began, people started pulling leaves and twigs from the tree as mementos. We thought it would be neat to actually touch the tree or sit beneath it since it is quite large. Debbie spotted a man mowing the area under the tree and went by the gate to get his attention and tell him we wanted to go through the fence. He was not amused and didn't let us go in. One of the few times ever that Debbie wasn't able to convince someone we had to be allowed to do something.

We were at the Cathedral of Santiago de Compostela in Spain on the Jubilee Year when they opened the

Holy Door of the Cathedral. Early one morning, we and a few others from the group were admitted to the tomb of St. James to celebrate Mass with Msgr. Swetland on the feast day of St. James. This is not something an ordinary visitor to the Cathedral is allowed to do. Then we snuck back to the group for breakfast before we departed.

Of course, personally knowing the family of Servant of God Maria Esperanza makes visiting *Betania*, Venezuela like no other pilgrimage. We are part of their family, and talking and praying with people who have actually seen Our Lady is a supernatural experience.

Even with all the time spent visiting the many holy sites, the pilgrimages were primarily a time of prayer and reflection. On many of them, prayer teams met with the other pilgrims on the trip. We had the opportunity to celebrate Mass or just sit and pray in the most holy places on earth. They were a great opportunity to reflect and be grateful for all of the people and blessings in our lives.

Chapter 10

Conclusion

It is inevitable that hosting literally hundreds of speakers over the years would lead to some instances where things were not right. Sometimes God teaches us lessons by letting us fall and get up again. Just as the evil one can masquerade as an angel of light, we have had some experiences where people were not as they presented themselves. We have learned the hard way that there are some people who do not want others to succeed or, because of jealousy or envy, purposely try to cause chaos or trouble. There are some who want to manipulate a situation to their own desires. While this may seem negative or judgmental, it is the concupiscence of man that causes sinfulness. Some of these people may even have felt they are doing good in their own minds. There are speakers that we have not allowed to return because they were not following the orthodoxy of the Church.

God has protected us along the way. We learned how to look more deeply into suggestions we are given, to examine and vet every priest and speaker we consider as a presenter. During the retreats, we discern what is being taught and make sure it is aligned 100% with the teachings of the Catholic Church. People have suggested certain topics or devotions to us over the years. We have a hard and fast rule: if it is not officially approved by the Church, we do not allow it.

The ministry has continued to grow. People find us when they are searching on the internet for Catholic conferences or specific priests. We receive prayer requests from people daily that ask us to publish them on our website or send them to our community members for prayer. We have a daily holy hour where someone prays for all priests. An important part of our ministry from the beginning is to support the priesthood, and we encourage that at every opportunity.

The internet has allowed us to have our sacramentals available online. The books and other sacramentals we have available have primarily been promoted to help others in their spiritual life. It is a way for us to supplement our income, but it is always with the intention to help others grow in their faith. That is our focus. Through our store, we have reached people literally around the world. We have sent out orders throughout the U.S., Canada, Australia, New Zealand and throughout Europe, including Croatia and Greece. Our sacramentals have traveled to Singapore, the Far East and India. Often, people thank us for making these items available to them as they do not have access to many of them.

We have worked for all of our 25 years of ministry trying to finance a ministry solely on donations; seeking out speakers and topics that are needed for the time and working and managing properties and people. We wouldn't trade our lives for anyone else's. We have traveled throughout the world, met people we would never have normally met, have known countless Bishops, priests and speakers that have inspired us, taught us and became our friends. We think of Mother Teresa, who said, "I am a pencil in the hand of God." God does all the work here. He has consistently sent the people we need to help us, provide for our finances (sometimes at the 11th hour), and pray for us. No one gives a pencil the credit for a book. We take no credit for the lives that have been forever changed through OSMM. God has been the author of all the fruits of our labor.

It is natural to wonder what our future holds. How

long does God want us to continue our ministry? All Christians have to question where this world is heading. The bond of a shared morality and common truth for people has been eroded away right before our eyes. Faith in God and in His Truth is needed as much now as it has ever been needed.

To put it simply, we don't know where the future will lead us. The one thing we do know is we will follow wherever the Lord leads us no matter how difficult or impossible it may seem. It is our "yes," our "fiat" to Him, our Creator. As the Virgin Mary gave her "Fiat" to the Archangel Gabriel, we give our "fiat" because we know God will provide the people, strength, courage and most importantly, the Grace to do His Holy Will.

Appendix i

Musings

- In the early days, we relied on mailings to promote our conference. Once, Vanessa had the entire floor at her home covered in brochures. It was a big area as there were over 25,000 flyers that had to be sorted in order to qualify for bulk mail rates. It took her a week to sort all of them out. When she went to the post office, they told her it was all wrong, and she literally sat in the post office for two consecutive days redoing all of it.

- During one of our early conferences, we had over ten speakers at our Annual Conference, all of them big names. One priest tore up his stipend check and sprinkled it in Debbie's hand because it was not made out to the proper entity. This involved arranging for people to pick up and deliver speakers at all hours to and from the airport 60 miles away.

- Like any group of people, there are priests who have lots of stipulations and requests and others who ask for nothing and appreciate everything. On one end of the spectrum, we had a particular priest who had to fly First Class, requested a certain type of tea and required many other amenities. On the other end is Fr. Emmerich Vogt, OP, who would get up early on the last day of the retreat, wash and dry the bed sheets and remake the bed. He would wash any dishes and clean the kitchen. When he left, it was like he had never even been there.

- When Fr. James LeBar was picked up at the airport, the vehicle of the person who picked him up was filled with the odor of excrement. Being an exorcist, Father remarked he was used to this type of thing as the evil one was making himself known. No big deal.

- One of the earliest speakers we hosted was Fr. Stan Fortuna, CFR. We literally chased Fr. Stan down the hall at a conference to invite him to come to our little town. He came to Vandalia twice and brought the Word of God through his music ministry, singing and playing his guitar.

- Debbie worked hard to get Fr. Benedict Groeschel CFR to come to Vandalia. It was one of the few times that we were not able to convince someone to come. We had seen him at many different events and really wanted him to come. When he saw us coming toward him at one event, a look of terror came over his face. When we spoke, he told us he knew who we were and what we wanted. He remained firm that he was not interested in coming to Vandalia.

- On a pilgrimage to the Holy Land as we approached Jericho, we passed a large hillside where a monastery is located on the Mt. of Temptation in the desert. The priest who was leading the pilgrimage still had some boyish impulses in him, and decided to slide several hundred feet down the sandy descent, and then had to hike along the bottom of the crevice to where he could climb back out. While we watched, he was nothing more than a dot in the distance. Needless to say, he made us late for our next destination as we waited for him to find his way back.

- On the Sea of Galilee, pilgrims are taken on "Jesus" boats that are constructed the same as the boats used by Peter and the apostles. Annie Karto and our priest for the trip, Fr. Andy Davey, began to lead us in song with their beautiful voices. Soon, we all circled around in the boat and began to sing and dance as we traveled over the gentle waves. It was a God-filled day.

- As we've mentioned, Vandalia is not a Catholic town. Seeing priests or nuns is far from the ordinary. But, Vandalia seems to take that a step further. Fr. Dubay was here with a group of priests for a private retreat, and they took an early morning walk to pray. Someone called the police on them because they looked suspicious.

A religious sister, who was here as a presenter, took a walk wearing her full habit, stopped to sit on a park bench and pray. It was not long before a police car with lights and siren approached and asked, "You are?" Her response, "A Catholic nun." He said, "Oh," and he left.

I guess with the growth of school shootings, people are more apt to be paranoid, but one of the priests who came to speak took a walk near the high school. It was winter, and he wore his cassock and had a long black coat over it. Someone drove by and called the police because they thought it might be a school shooter. The police were once again able to keep our town safe!

There are people in town who have sworn they have seen nuns waving out the windows of Bethany House. We are not sure what they are seeing, but we can assure everyone that no Sisters have ever lived there, and if they had, we don't believe they would spend their time waving out the windows.

- Before we built the Sanctuary we would store all of our items for retreats at a local storage unit. This was usually accomplished by piling as much as we could into cars and pick-ups trucks to try and cut down on the numerous trips it would require. We drew a lot of attention when two of our community members rode on the tailgate of a truck holding on to the statues of the Archangels as they drove down the street.

- When we first contact people to speak at our events, many of them assume we are nuns and refer to us as Sister... Even when we correct them and say we are just lay people, they keep referring to us as Sister.

- For some reason, many of our speakers cannot remember the name of the ministry. We have been called. Our Lady's Sorrows, Our Lady of Sorrows, Our Mother's Sorrows. All kinds of combinations of our name have been used.

- We have had the privilege of working with Chris DeShazo, who has painted many of the images on the walls of our chapel and the Sanctuary. She has also restored many statues for us. When Chris was painting the *Agnus Dei* lamb on the wall in Mary's Chapel, she stopped and told us she was experiencing a miracle. She had measured segments around a large circle completely freehand. When she got to the end, the measurement was exactly what all of the others were. She said that NEVER happens. You can see Chris' incredible talent throughout Mary's Chapel as it is painted to resemble the ancient catacombs in Rome and the larger-than-life-size images of St. Michael, St. Gabriel and St. Raphael. Chris did all of the lettering in the Sanctuary and painted the *Fleur de li*s in the *Stabat Mater Dolorosa*.

- We are surrounded by the work of Gary from Wisconsin, who came and spent a week at the Sanctuary building and painting the tabernacle, all of the shelving that holds the statues of the saints, and constructed the crucifix for a large corpus of Christ someone gave us. He and his wife rebuilt and touched up the gold on the main altar of the sanctuary that we were able to salvage from a convent of Mother Cabrini.

- A man told us about a statue of the Dying St. Joseph that he would be able to get for us. It was located at the Pious Union of St. Joseph in

Grass Lake, Michigan. He had made arrangements for a statue that had some damage to be donated to us. Our friend Bill drove up there to retrieve the statue, and when he got there, the pastor had changed his mind, and he gave us another image of the Dying St. Joseph. This one was in perfect condition. He got a lot of quizzical looks from other drivers as he drove back to Vandalia with a large statue of St. Joseph reclining with Mary and Jesus surrounding him in the back of a truck. This statue became one of our favorites.

- This same friend Bill once came to us and told us that while he was traveling, he thought Our Lady had stopped him on the road and told him to go to a casino and give us his winnings. We didn't know what to think when he handed us $2700. Not sure if it was right or not to accept the money, we placed it beneath a statue of the Blessed Mother in Mary's Chapel. Strangely enough, we completely forgot about it. Many years later, Chris, our painter, moved the statue to paint and discovered the money. Our Lady had safeguarded it for us.

- We had a retreat on Sunday, April 22, 2007, and the Gospel reading at Mass was about the Apostles catching 153 fish. The money we received in the collection was exactly $153. God has a good sense of humor.

- On one of the first attempts to provide exorcised water to everyone at a retreat, someone had used a dirty trash can at the Junior High. Ted and Randy were hurriedly trying to fill jugs with the water, and a lady came up, and before they could stop her, scooped up a cup of the dirty water and drank it down!!

- We have a devotion to the Holy Souls and scheduled Fr. Anthony Gramlich, MIC for a retreat on the Holy Souls in Purgatory. When we got closer to the date, we realized that the retreat was on November 16th, the feast day of St. Gertrude the Great, who is the Patroness of Holy Souls. Many of you are familiar with her prayer: *Eternal Father, I offer Thee the Most Precious Blood of Thy Divine Son, Jesus, in union with the Masses said throughout the world today, for all the holy souls in purgatory, for sinners everywhere, for sinners in the universal church, those in my own home and within my family. Amen.*

Appendix ii

Our Sorrowful Mother's Ministry Events

1997

October 20 & 21 Mon. & Tues. – Fr. Peter Rookey

1998

January 20 & 21 Tues. & Wed. — Fr. Tom McCarthy

March 29 Sunday– Fr. Andy Lewandowski & Shepherd's Voice

May 22 & 23 Fri. & Sat. – Fr. Stan Fortuna CFR

June 15 Mon. — Fr. Roberto Ike

October 2, 3 & 4 Fri., Sat. & Sun. — First Annual Conference - Marian Conference-Fr. Peter Rookey, Msgr. Francis Friedl, Dana, Fr. Stan Fortuna CFR, Fr. Milton Thomas, Jill & Brent Hammachek, Katy Feeney

November 9, Mon. — Fr. Peter Rookey

1999

February 2 Tues.—Our Lady of Fatima Pilgrim Statue

March 26 & 27 Fri. & Sat.—Eucharistic Apostles of the Divine Mercy

April 12 & 13 Mon. & Tues.—Life Foundation

July 7 & 8 Wed. & Thur.—Fr. Andrew John Winchek

July 16 & 17 Fri. & Sat.—Bruce Sullivan

October 30 & 31—2nd Annual Conference - Apologetics Conference-Karl Keating, Tim Staples, Steve Ray, David Currie, Dr. Kenneth Howell, Fr. John Capuci, Archbishop Joseph Naumann, Zip Rzeppa, Emma Deguzman, Life Foundation, Fr. Andrew John Winchek, Annie Karto

2000

October 27, 28 & 29, 3rd Annual-Celebrate the Faith Conference "You are a Priest Forever" Fr. John Corapi, Fr. Bill Casey CPM, Fr. James Lebar, Fr. Jordan Aumann, Fr. Philip Scott, Fr. Tom McCarthy, Fr. Ken Hummel, Fr. Peter West, Zip Rzeppa, Annie Karto

Dec. 6 -Tim Staples

2001

March 30 & 31 — Healing Your Family Tree Retreat w/Fr. John Hampsch

May 18 & 19 — Firewalk of Faith Retreat w/Alex Jones, Msgr. Stuart Swetland, Fr. Tony Dittmer, Donna Jones, Apostles of the Interior Life

October 26, 27 & 28 — 4th Annual Conference - Celebrate the Faith Conference-"Do you love Me-Feed My Sheep — Bishop George Lucas, Msgr. Stuart Swetland, Fr. Stephen Sotiroff, Fr. Mitch Pacwa, Fr. Joseph Fessio, Fr. Peter Stravinskas, Fr. Stan Fortuna CFR, Rosalind Moss, Alex Jones, Fr. Philip Scott, Fr. Peter Rookey, Apostles of the Interior Life, Jill Stanek, Juraj, Firewalk Music

2002

March 8 & 9 – Lenten Retreat w/Companions of the Cross-Fr. Jon Vandenakker

April 29, 30 & May 1 — Fr. Thomas Dubay Retreat

June 14-24-Italy Pilgrimage: Msgr. Swetland, Apostles of the Interior Life

August 3-Fr. Clement Machado

October 25, 26 & 27-Celebrate the Faith/5th Annual- "Put on the Armor of God"-Fr. James LeBar, Mother Nadine Brown, Fr. Tom Euteneur, Alex Jones, Fr. Bill Casey CPM, Msgr. Stuart Swetland, Fr. Philip Scott, Apostles of the Interior Life

November 15 & 16-Emma de Guzman

2003

February 7, 8 & 9-Fr. John Hampsch, Sr. Ann Shields- Pre-Lenten Healing Your Family Tree.

May 19, 20, 21-Fr. Thomas Dubay Retreat

May 27-June 6-Italy Pilgrimage

August 8 &9-Fr. Clement Machado Retreat

October 24, 25, 26-Celebrate the Faith/6th Annual- "Behold I stand at the Door and Knock"-Msgr. Stuart Swetland, Bishop David Ricken, Fr. Stephen Sotiroff, Karl Keating, Fr. Philip Scott, Patrick Madrid, Johnette Benkovic, Patty Schneier, Dr. Kenneth Howell, Apostles of the Interior Life, Annie Karto, Radix

November 7 & 8, 2003-Why Be Catholic? –Msgr. Swetland, Rosalind Moss

December 30, 2003- Fr. Machado

2004

March 18-24 -Spain/Fatima Pilgrimage

April 23, 24 & 25-Family, Faith & Culture w/Fr. Philip Scott, Mother Mary Elizabeth & Dr. Mike Gonzales

May 24 - June 5—Italy Pilgrimage, Msgr. Swetland

July 9, 10 & 11-Fr. Clement Machado Retreat

Aug. 13, 14 & 15-Fr. Clement Machado Retreat

Sept. 5, 2004-Benefit for Fr. Machado's ministry

October 29, 30 & 31 7th Annual Conference - Celebrate the Faith conference-"The Year of the Eucharist-Starting Afresh from Christ"-Fr. Frank Pavone, Fr. Bill Casey CPM, Fr. Philip Scott, Msgr. Stuart Swetland, Abbot John Klassen, OSB, Rosalind Moss, Apostles of the Interior Life

2005

March 18, 19, 20-Fr. Leo Maasburg

April 15, 16, 17-St. Gianna Beretta Molla — Jim Buffler

June 10, 11 & 12-Retreat w/Fr. Philip Scott, Mother Mary Elizabeth & Mike Gonzalez

June 20-July 3-Italy Pilgrimage, Msgr. Swetland

August 5, 6 & 7-Retreat w/Fr. Pablo Straub & Fr. Chris Crotty, CPM

September 30-Oct. 1-Retreat w/Msgr. Frank Chiodo and Sr. Louis Montfort

October 28, 29 & 30- 8th Annual Conference - Celebrate the Faith Conference-"Come to Me all you who labor and are burdened, and I will give you rest."--Msgr. Stuart Swetland, Fr. Andrew Apostoli CFR, Fr. Delix Michel, Moira Noonan, Randall Sullivan, Fr. Anthony Buse`, Fr. Philip Scott, Apostles of the Interior Life

December 1,2 & 3-Healing Retreat w/Fr. Christopher Crotty, CPM

2006

February 24-26-Healing Retreat w/Fr. David Wilton

Holy Land Pilgrimage 3/16-3/26

May 26-28-Healing Retreat w/Fr. Christopher Crotty, CPM

September 8-10-Healing & Deliverance Retreat w/Fr. Chris Crotty, CPM

October 27-29-Celebrate the Faith 9th Annual-"Only say the Word and I shall be Healed"--Msgr. Stuart Swetland, Gianna Jessen, Theresa Grentz, Fr. Bill Casey CPM, Fr. Christopher Crotty, Fr. Philip Scott, Apostles of the Interior Life

November 10-12- Healing & Deliverance Retreat w/Fr. Chris Crotty

2007

January 19-21-Healing Retreat-Fr. Mark Baron MIC/Moira Noonan, Rob Abel

February 16-18- Healing Retreat-Fr. Pablo Straub, Fr. David Wilton

March 16-18-"Come to the Cross" Lenten Retreat-Fr. Mark Baron MIC

April 20-22-Healing Retreat-Fr. John Larson, Apostles of the Interior Life

June 29-July 1-Womens' Humor & Healing Retreat-Fr. Mark Baron MIC, Theresa Grentz

July 20-22-Intensive Family Tree Healing-Fr. Zachary, Fr. John Titus

August 17-19- Healing Retreat-Fr. Pablo Straub, Fr. Bill Casey CPM

September 7-9- 1st Anniversary of Mary's Chapel- Family Tree & Inner Healing Retreat-Fr. Bill McCarthy & Mary Alice Rossini

October 26-28- 10th Annual Conference - "Lord, Heal the Broken-Hearted"- Fr. Mark Baron MIC, Theresa Grentz,

The Apostles of the Interior Life, Fr. Richard McAlear, Fr. Andrew Apostoli, CFR Bishop George Lucas, Fr. Delix Michel, Fr. John Titus, Annie Karto & Matthew Baute.

November 22-Dec. 1—Pilgrimage to the Holy Land, Msgr. Swetland

2008

January 18-20-Fr. Mariutsz, Fr. John Titus-"Deep Healing in the Ocean of God's Mercy"

February 15-17-Fr. Mark Baron, Fr. John Titus-"Hold Me Lord; Healing the Whole Person(Family Tree Healing Weekend)

March 14-16-Fr. Joe Whalen, Fr. John Titus, Mary Ann Wichmann

April-Trip to MFH for retreat and to NY for Pope Benedict XVI visit.

June 20-22-Fr. Bill McCarthy, Mary Alice Rossini, Fr. John Larson- "School of Healing"

August 22-24-Fr. Joe Whalen, Fr. John Titus, Mary Ann Wichmann-"Inner Healing thru Our Lady of Reconciliation"

September 5-7- Fr. Meinrad Miller "Healing the Hearts Wounds"

September 19-21-Fr. Philip Chavez-Celebration for Our Sorrowful Mother, St. Januarius & Our Lady of LaSalette feast days

October 31, November 1& 2-11 th Annual Conference - Fr. Joe Whalen, Fr. Bill Casey CPM, Sr. Rosalind Moss, Splat, St. Luke Productions (Story of St. Therese), Apostles of the Interior Life

November 9-22-Pilgrimage to the Holy Land, Fr. Mark Baron, MIC

2009

January 2-4-Fr. Patrick Greenough—"Getting to Know Mary"

February 6-8-Fr. Anthony Gramlich MIC—"Holy Souls in Purgatory"

March 27-29-Fr. Wolfgang Seitz-"Living with the Holy Angels"

April 24 & 25-Msgr. John Esseff & Dr. Richard Gallagher-"Spiritual Warfare"

June 26-28-Fr. Tony Dittmer & Dr. Richard Meyer

July 17-19-Fr. Dwight Longenecker & John LaBriola

August 7-9-Fr. Andrew Apostoli CFR

September 4-6-Fr. Mark Baron MIC, Dr. Richard

Meyer & Epiphany Productions-"Allesandro"

September 18-20-Fr. Dwight Longenecker & John LaBriola

October 30-Nov. 1-12th Annual Conference -Msgr. Stuart Swetland, Fr. Emmerich Vogt OP, Fr. Bill Casey CPM, Chuck Neff, Apostles of the Interior Life, Splat

Nov 30-Dec 12--Holy Land Pilgrimage with Fr. Mark Baron MIC

2010

January 15-17-Community Retreat w/Fr. Anthony Gramlich MIC

February 26-28-Fr. Michael Lightner

March 19-21-Fr. Wolfgang Seitz-Opus Sanctorum Angelorum

April 23-25-Fr. Jose Antonio Fortea, Dr. Richard Gallagher

June 4-6-Fr. Emmerich Vogt OP

June 11-23 — Pilgrimage with Msgr. Stuart Swetland--

Santiago de Compostela. Ars, LaSalette, Lourdes, Avila, Fatima (Year of the Priest)

July 23-24--Fr. Bill McCarthy & Mary Alice Rossini

September 17-19 — Fr. Mark Baron MIC

Oct. 29-31-13th Annual Conference-- Msgr. Stewart Swetland, S.T.D., Fr. James Albers, OSM, Fr. William Halbing,

Rebecca Kiessling, Randy Albright, Apostles of the Interior Life

November 28-December 11-Pilgrimage with Fr. Mark Baron MIIC to the Holy Land

2011

January — Fr. Bill McCarthy, Mary Alice Rossini, Dr. Kevin Vost

February--Fr. Richard McAlear, Fr. Martin, Vicki Thorn

April — Fr. Greg Cleveland

May — Fr. Mark Baron MIC

May 31-June 13-- Pilgrimage to Fatima, Lourdes, Laus, LaSalette

July 15-17-Community Retreat-Fr. Andrew Apostoli CFR

July 22-24 — Fr. Anthony Gramlich MIC

August 3& 4 — 6 & 7 — Msgr. Stuart Swetland and Fr. Ermelindo

August 19-21 — Fr. Joe Whalen & Fr. John Welch

September 9-11 — Fr. Mark Baron MIC

October 28-30 — 14th Annual Conference -Mike Roberts, Fr. Philip Scott, Fr. Stefan Starcynski, Fr. Bill Casey CPM, Bishop Thomas John Paprocki, Apostles of the Interior Life

November 11-13 — Fr. Tim Byerley & Family of Maria Esperanza and Betania foundation

2012

January 22-24 — Fr. Bob Vennetti & John Garcia

February 24-26 — Community Retreat — Fr. Andrew Apostoli CFR & Dr. Margarett Schlientz

April 13-15 — Divine Mercy — Fr. Martin

April 27-29 — Healing the Father & Mother Wound — Fr. Philip Scott

June 8 & 9 — Mark Mallett

June 19 & 20 — True Forgiveness & Healing — Fr. Ubald

June 22-24 — True Forgiveness & Healing — Fr. Ubald

June 24 — Grand Opening and Blessing by Bishop of the Sanctuary of the Sorrowful Mother

Aug 14, 21 & 22 — Public veneration of St. Pio relics 10am-2pm & 5pm-8pm

August 15 & 16 — Fr. Ermelindo — St. Padre Pio

August 17-19 — Fr. Ermelindo — St. Padre Pio

September 7-9 — Fr. Philip Scott — Healing the Family

September 14-16 — Fr. Mark Baron MIC — OLO Sorrows and OLO LaSalette Feasts

October 26-28 — 15th Annual Conference — Msgr. Stuart Swetland, Fr. Ubald, Immaculee Ilibagiza, Apostles of the Interior Life

November 16-18 — Fr. Anthony Gramlich MIC — Poor Souls in Purgatory

2013

January 18 & 19 — Fr. Peter Stryker — OLO Good Help — Hope, Healing, Forgiveness & Miracles

February 1 & 2 — Fr. Martin — Faith in a Faithless World

March 1 & 2 — Fr. Seraphim Michalenko, MIC Fr. Henry Ussher — Forgive the Unforgivable

March 18 — St. Mary Magdalene Relic

April 5-7 — Fr. George

April 19 & 20 — Fr. Richard McAlear OMI & Fr. Patrick — Speaking From the Heart-Hope, Healing & Forgiveness

July 5 & 6 — Fr. Anthony Gramlich MIC & Srs. Of Mercy — Healing & Forgiveness thru Divine Mercy & St. Faustina and the Diary

July 12 & 13 — Fr. Harold Imamshah — Healing the Father & Mother Wound

September 6 & 7 — Fr. Mark Baron MIC — Discernment of Spirits

September 13 & 14 – Fr. Joseph Christensen – Enter Into the Mysteries & Promises of Our Sorrowful Mother

September 20 & 21 – Fr. Philip Scott – Healing the Father & Mother Wound

October 18 & 19 – Fr. Andrew Apostoli CFR & Franciscan Sisters of the Renewal – OLO Fatima-Our Last Refuge

October 25-27 – 16th Annual Conference Betania Representatives-Coky, Piri, Abraham, Dulce, Frank, Maria Francia, Carolina, Fr. Bill Casey CPM, Fr. Tom Sullivan CPM, Apostles of the Interior Life, Chuck Neff, Annie Karto & Matthew Baute

November 8 & 9 – Fr. Emmerich Vogt OP

November 22 & 23 – Fr. Andrew Apostoli CFR, Kathleen McCarthy

2014

January 17 & 18 – Fr. Bob Vennetti MIC, & Kathleen McCarthy

January --Betania

February 7 & 8 — Fr. Peter Stryker & Michael O'Neill

February 21 & 22 — Fr. Chad Ripperger & Dr. Margarett Schlientz

March 7 & 8 — Fr. Daniel Balizan

March 21-23 — Fr. Stefan Starzynski & Howard Storm

April 4 & 5 — Fr. Aniello Salicone & Kathleen McCarthy

May 2 & 3 — Fr. Peter West, Bishop Paprocki & Linda Santo-Icon of OLO Częstochowa

July 18 & 19 — Fr. Glenn Sudano, CFR, Ramona Trevino & Faustina Drama w/Nancy Scimone

August 1 & 2 — Fr. Jim McCormack MIC, & Kathleen McCarthy

September 5 & 6 -- Fr. Emmerich Vogt OP & Rosario Rodriguez

September 19 & 20 -- Msgr. Stuart Swetland & Francisciscan Sisters, T.O.R. of Penance of the Sorrowful Mother

October 31, November 1 & 2 — 17th Annual

Conference--Bishop Paprocki, Joseph Pearce, Fr. Peter/Poland, Apostles of the Interior Life, Betania Family

December 5-7--Fr. Philip Scott, FJH

December 7-12 — Betania Pilgrimage

2015

January 23 & 24--Fr. Aniello Salicone

February 7 & 8 — Fr. Glenn Sudano CFR

March 6 & 7 — Fr. Chad Ripperger

March 22-28 — Betania Pilgrimage

April 10 & 11 — Fr. Aniello Salicone

July 10 & 11 — Fr. Chad Ripperger

August 5-12 — Betania Pilgrimage

August 21 & 22 — Fr. Glenn Sudano CFR

Oct. 30-Nov. 1-18th Annual Conference--Bishop Paprocki, Fr. Bill Casey CPM, 37 Members of the Betania Family, Apostles of the Interior Life

November 20 & 21-Fr. Lou Cerulli

Dec. 4 & 5-Fr. Chad Ripperger

2016

Jan. 8-10--Fr. Chad Ripperger & Fr. Daniel McElheron

February 26 & 27 – Fr. Chad Ripperger

Feb. 29-Mar. 4-Fr. Daniel McElheron. – Deliverance Week

March 18 & 19--Fr. Chad Ripperger

April 22-24--St. Pope John Paul II relics, Bishop Thomas John Paprocki & Michael Brown

April 25-29-Fr. Daniel McElheron – Deliverance Week

May 16-20 – Intercessors Workshop – Kyle Clement

June 21-24 – Fr. Chad Ripperger & Kyle Clement – Deliverance Week

July 22 & 23--Fr. Chad Ripperger

August 3-12 – Betania

September 30-Oct. 2. — Fr. Chad Ripperger-Deliverance sessions

Oct. 3-6 — Fr. Chad Ripperger--Private retreat

Oct. 7-9 — Fr. Chad Ripperger

Oct. 28-30 — 19th Annual Conference/Bishop Paprocki, Fr. Peter/Poland, Betania Family, Apostles of the Interior Life (October 23-Nov. 2nd Family of Maria Esperanza at OSMM/Betania XVI)

Nov. 3-8 — Fr. Chad Ripperger — Deliverance Week

Dec. 7-16--Betania pilgrimage

2017

Feb. 17-19 — Fr. Anthony Gramlich MIC — The 7 Sorrows of Our Lady

March 17-19 — Fr. Aniello Salicone

April 19-28 — Betania pilgrimage

May 15-19 — Fr. Chad Ripperger — Deliverance Week

May 19-21 — Fr. Chad Ripperger — How to Spiritually Navigate the Problems in the World & the Church

July 7-9 — Fr. Jim McCormack MIC

July 28-30 — Fr. Ben Luedtke & John LaBriola — Forgive that you Might be Forgiven

August 25-27 — Fr. Elias Mills

September 29-Oct. 1 — Fr. Peter Glas & Fr. Kostrzewa The Truth Will Set You Free

October 27-29 — 20th Annual Conference — Archbishop Joseph Naumann, Fr. Bill Casey CPM, Dan Burke & Apostles of the Interior Life

December 6-15--Betania Pilgrimage

2018

January 26-28 Fr. Anthony Gramlich MIC, Marian Apparitions, Finding Truth and Grace

February 9-11, Fr. Lawrence Carney, Walking the Road to God and Out of the Darkness

March Betania Pilgrimage

April 27-29, Fr. Paul Desmarais, From Hope to Healing

July 13-15, Fr. Ben Luedtke, John LaBriola, Protection and Healing from the Spiritual Darkness Around Us

July 27-29, Fr. Mike Driscoll, Demons, Deliverance and Discernment: Separating Fact from Fiction about the Spirit World

October 26-28 - 21st Annual Conference: Lord, Come and Prepare Us for Battle, Bishop Thomas John Paprocki, Fr. Wade Menezes, CPM, Msgr. C. Eugene Morris, Sr. Susan Pieper

2019

February 8-10, Fr. James W. Jackson, Nothing Superfluous

March 15-17 Fr. Ben Luedtke, The Ripple Effect of Sexual Sin

March 29-31 Msgr. C. Eugene Morris, Grief and Suffering

April 12-14 Fr. Aniello Salicone Unforgiveness

April 26-28 Fr. Shannon Collins, David L. Gray Suffering

July 19-21 Fr. David Jenuwine Opposing the Mystery of Iniquity: Spiritual Advice for Catholics in the 21st century

September 20-22 Fr. Jim McCormick, MIC Consoling the Heart of Jesus

October 25-27 22rd Annual Conference Political Correctness and the Cross of Social Martyrdom Bishop Thomas John Paprocki, Fr. Bill Casey, CPM, David L. Gray, Sr. Susan Pieper

2020

February 13-14, Fr. Jacques Philippe, Inner Peace, Sr. Susan Pieper

July 17-19 Fr. Shannon Collins Our Lady of Sorrows Co-Redemptrix

August 1 Christine Watkins, Kendra Von Esh, The Warning and the Illumination of Conscience

August 7-9 Fr. Joseph Esper Preparing for the Coming Persecution

September 18-20 Msgr. C. Eugene Morris, Depression, Anxiety, Trauma and Addiction from the Results of Woundedness

October 30-November 1 23rd Annual Conference Hold Fast to the One, True Faith, Bishop Thomas John Paprocki, Fr. Ignatius Manfredonia, F.I., Sr. Susan Pieper, Patricia Sandoval, David L. Gray, Kendra Von Esh.

2021

February 26-28 Fr. Joseph Tuscan Confraternity of Chrisitan Mothers Holiness: the path to Hope and the Role of Forgiveness in Relationships

March 19-21 Fr. Joseph Kuhlman St, Joseph as Father, Husband: Fulfillment of Prophecy and Providence for Our Times

June 25-27 Fr. James Blount, SOLT

July 9-11 Fr. Paul Desmarais, Pamela Acker Divine Mercy in Deliverance Ministry

September 17-19 Fr. Shannon Collins, MSJB St. Joseph and the Family

October 29-31 24th Annual Conference Bishop

Thomas John Paprocki, Msgr. Eugene Morris, Fr. Quan Tran, Patricia Sandoval, Pamela Acker, Sr. Susan Pieper

2022

February 25-27 Fr. Shannon Collins, MSJB Restoring the Sacred

Mar. 18-20 Fr. Joseph Kuhlmann , Jeannie Ewing The Transfiguration of Suffering

April 1-3 Fr. Ambrose Criste, O. Praem The Ministry of the Guardian Angels

April 30 Fr. Ripperger

July 22-24 Fr. Rick Heilman
Truth & Perseverance — The two powerful virtues the devil hates

Aug. 5-7 Fr. Joseph Esper, John LaBriola
Jesus vs Satan in 21st Century America

Oct. 28-30 25th Annual Conference: Bishop Thomas John Paprocki, Fr. Bill Casey,
Msgr. Swetland, Fr. Stephen Sotiroff, Sr. Susan

Pieper, Fr. Seth Brown, Fr. John Titus, Leah Darrow/Augustine Institute, John LaBriola As the Family Goes, So Goes the Whole World in which We Live

Acknowledgments

A special thank you to:

We are forever grateful to Ann Stock and Mariann Timmermann for their faithful support every day, day in and day out. They do a myriad of tasks too numerous to list. Without their help and dedication, we could not run this ministry. They are such an integral part of what is accomplished here. We are so very thankful for them.

We want to thank all of our community members for the ways in which they help OSMM to keep growing.

We would like to thank Ann for taking the time, effort and dedication to collect our memories and the journey we have been on with OSMM for 25 years. She has expertly arranged all of it, and that is why we are able to share this book with you now. This feat has been attempted several times over the years, but she has completed it. Thank you, Ann. We know this has been a daunting task, and we are so grateful.

Our forever thanks to Mariann and Ann for their daily support, encouragement and never-ending jobs that make it all come together!

We could not have done this ministry without their daily commitment to this service.

They are truly servants.

With our love and gratitude…

All Glory, Honor and Thanksgiving to God for the great gift of allowing us to serve.

Fiat,

Debbie & Vanessa

Made in the USA
Monee, IL
22 September 2022